Lessons of Loss
A Guide to Coping

Robert A. Neimeyer
University of Memphis

D1715995

To my mother, Nan Neimeyer,
whose courage to survive in the wake of loss
inspired this book and the life work it represents.

For Additional Copies:
Center of the Study of Loss and Transition
P.O. Box 770656
Memphis, TN 38177-0656
901.849.4680
kestory@bellsouth.net

Contents

Preface

How can we understand the meaning of loss? In everyday speech, we associate it with being deprived of something that one has had (as in the loss of friends), with failure to keep or get something we value (as in the loss caused by a robbery), with a measurable reduction in some substance or process (as in loss of ability); and with destruction or ruin (as in the losses brought about by war). Clearly, loss can have many meanings, ranging from the agreed upon public definitions outlined above, with their reference to deprivation, failure, reduction and destruction, to the highly personal and perhaps inexpressible meanings associated with past and present losses in our own lives.

This book is about those losses, how we react to them, and how we can come to adapt to them. It acknowledges the many forms of loss in human life—through death, disease, and disability; through destruction of one's home, property, or career; and through dissolution of marriages, friendships, and other intimate relationships. Yet in spite of the diversity of these losses, there are some core similarities in the ways in which persons affected by them grieve. We will explore both the common themes and challenges that characterize the human experience of loss, and the special problems posed by particular losses as a result of how, when, and where they occur. While the pain of mourning that which we loved but no longer have is a natural part of the journey of life, it can nonetheless challenge our existing ways of living, leaving us confused and unsure of how to progress through the uncharted territory into which we are thrust by loss. My goal in these pages will be to describe the general contours of mourning, not only in terms of the bereaved individuals, but also in terms of their impact on the relationships in which we are embedded. Equally important, I will discuss ways of coping with major losses that leave us forever transformed, including resources that can contribute to the deepening of our lives, our selves, and our life philoso-phies. While no book can provide a universally valid "road map" of the pro-cess of mourning, I hope that the information and ideas in the pages that follow will help you understand and accommodate both your own experi-ences of loss, and the losses of those to whom you extend a helping hand on their journeys toward healing.

How to Use This Book

Most books about grief and loss are written at one of two levels. On the one hand, those written for lay readers have the advantage of readability, but too frequently offer simple formulas and generalizations that fail to respect the subtleties of loss and mourning, and occasionally insult the intelligence of their readers. On the other hand, texts written for professional audiences typically have the advantage of being grounded in research, but are often so academic in style that they fail either to convey the lived experience of griev-ing, or to interpret research results in a way that considers their implications for coping with bereavement. Thus, the first type of book may fall short by being too concrete and prescriptive, whereas the second may tend to be too abstract to have much practical value.

My solution to this dilemma has been to write at an intermediate level, in a way that I hope will be accessible to both professional helpers and intel-ligent lay readers. As a "thanatologist"—someone who studies death and dying—as a psychologist who counsels the bereaved, and as a person who acknowledges the role of loss in his own life, I have drawn equally on re-search and scholarship, clinical experience, and personal contact with loss in an effort to understand the nuances of grief with the head as well as the heart. This book is the result of this effort to distill some practical tools and guide-lines for coping with loss without denying its impact.

The chapters of this book are divided into three broad sections. The first part, entitled *For Those Who Grieve*, introduces the experience of loss, describes the anatomy of grief in broad brush strokes, and raises the ques-tion of when it is wise to reach for assistance beyond one's network of friends and family. It also considers the special challenges of job loss and relationship loss through divorce and departure, introduces the concept of meaning-making, and offers reflections on personal, social, and spiritual means of transcending the pain associated with bereavement. Because the pangs of acute grief disrupt even the most focused attention, I have intentionally kept individual chapters within this section short, interspersing them with numerous practical guidelines that can help us begin to understand how we cope with the losses in our lives. These chapters also offer a broad range of brief examples and illustrations to help build a bridge between the experience of bereavement and its conceptualization. Readers who have suffered a recent loss may find it most helpful to browse through this section, focusing attention on those chapters, issues, or guidelines that speak most directly to them, and moving ahead to the remainder of the book as time and concentration permit. Helping professionals should also find Part 1 useful in providing a readable summary of some major themes and findings concerning grief. In addition to their information value, the chapters making up this first section of the book might also serve as supportive readings and "homework assignments" for the bereaved clients served by grief therapists.

The second part of the book, entitled *For Those Who Help,* contains somewhat lengthier chapters that more fully present the model of *grieving as a process of meaning reconstruction,* a framework that is alluded to in Part 1. While the language used to refer to such meaning making processes differs from one theorist to another, a concern with the way in which different bereaved persons find sense in their experience is shared by many clinicians and scholars on the "leading edge" of grief theory. The chapters in Part 2 offer more substantial case studies, and go into greater detail about the limitations of familiar stage models of grieving, the need for a fresh understanding of loss, and some propositions that might move us toward such an understanding. Most important, they offer a new vision of what it might mean to help those who grieve, and set the stage for a discussion of therapeutic tasks that flow from this new way of thinking about a familiar problem. While the ideas and case studies contained in this section are written explicitly with the grief counselor in mind, they are also intended to speak to the bereaved individual who is looking both for the larger meanings of loss, and a way of putting it in perspective. Thus, just as I hope Part 1 will represent useful supplemental reading for the grief professional, I hope that Part 2 will offer something of value to bereaved persons, a category that ultimately includes us all.

Finally, the third and final section of the book, entitled **Personal Resources,** speaks equally to both sets of potential readers. The first lengthy chapter in this section distills the abstract themes of meaning reconstruction into dozens of personal applications and variations, which promote greater articulation and acceptance of our changed status as a result of bereavement, foster a continued and constructive connection to those we have lost, and encourage appropriate memorialization of those we have loved. The many exercises described in this chapter, ranging from loss journals and memory books to metaphoric narratives and personal rituals, can be used either as guides to self-help and self-reflection, or as therapeutic "homework" in the context of grief counseling. However, I recognize that the written text ultimately can provide only so much support for those who have suffered loss, and can rarely replace the direct person-to-person contact needed to help a person whose world has collapsed to again feel integrated into a community of care. Likewise, no book can substitute for serious training in newer approaches to grief counseling for helping professionals who wish to become better versed in these ideas and methods. Thus, I have tried to offer contact information for a few of the many support organizations and professional associations that can provide such services. For this reason, the book concludes with a resource directory pointing the interested reader to other books, Internet sites, and organizations that can be of assistance to both bereaved individuals and professional helpers.

A further point concerns my style of referring to other literature in the pages that follow. In striving for readability, I decided to forego the usual in-text citations of journal articles, books, and chapters that crowd their way into most academic prose. However, I recognize that many readers, lay and professional alike, will be interested in the original sources of the ideas offered in this book, or simply in using this book as a jumping off point into a broad and fascinating literature contributing to new models of grief and loss. For these readers I have included numerous **Research Notes** at the end of each chapter, which offer a bit more detail and appropriate citations to the primary and secondary source material most directly relevant to the content of the chapter. However, in a book of this scope, I have made no attempt to be comprehensive, and I would refer the reader to the bibliography of suggested scientific and applied publications provided at the end of the book for more exhaustive treatments of many of the issues raised in these pages.

In closing, I hope that you as a reader will find something of value in these pages, whether you are a helping professional hoping to hone your clinical skills and sensitivities in working with the many faces of loss, someone whose own life has been touched by loss and is on the journey toward renewal, or both. Just as all grievers are potential (if informal) helpers, all helpers also grieve. If some of the ideas or suggestions that follow contribute to your comfort, compassion, or comprehension of loss as a personal experience, my goal as an author will be met.

Robert A. Neimeyer, Ph.D.
February, 1998

Part 1:

For Those Who Grieve

Chapter 1

The Experience of Loss

are the shadow of all possessions—material and immaterial.
Carlos Sluzki, family therapist

verything you have like precious china, because someday it will be gone.
Diana Bradley, survivor of the April 19, 1995,
Oklahoma City bombing, who lost her mother,
two children, and right leg in the blast

A middle-aged woman is widowed by the sudden heart attack of her husband of over 20 years, the father of her three young children. A young mother and father are left bereft and devastated by the inexplicable "crib death" of their infant daughter. A California family is forced to move when a catastrophic mudslide destroys their crops and home. A community and an entire nation is left shocked, outraged, and insecure following a senseless terrorist bombing of a federal office complex, taking the lives of scores of children and adults.

The losses occasioned by events like these are only the most visible of those we encounter in the course of life. Others are subtler, less socially sanctioned, or more "hidden." An executive becomes depressed and self-critical following his termination from his job due to company "downsizing." A young man feels betrayed and angry when his girlfriend leaves him for another man. An unwed mother-to-be mourns the loss of her unborn child as a result of a spontaneous miscarriage. A family feels stigmatized and avoided following the suicide of one of its members. A gay man feels marginalized and scapegoated when he is prevented from attending the funeral service for his partner arranged by his partner's parents. A child feels hurt and upset when his parents try to assuage his grief over his dead puppy by offering him a replacement. The grief triggered by such losses may be compounded by the misunderstanding, blame, or simple inattention of other people in the family, workplace or community, adding a burden of private anguish, secrecy, or shame for those whose mourning is disallowed, trivialized, or unrecognized by those around them. [1]

To more fully understand the experience of loss, it is helpful to recognize its universality in human life. In a sense, we lose something at each step along life's journey, from the concrete losses of people, places, and objects we have come to cherish, to the more immaterial but equally significant forfeiture of our youth, dreams, or ideals as we confront life's hard "realities." Even the positive transitions of our lives are not unmixed blessings, as each job promotion stresses established friendships, the birth of a child deprives new parents of taken-for-granted freedoms, the acceptance of children at a college of their choice confronts parents with the loneliness of an "empty nest," and the wished-for dissolution of a loveless relationship leads to complicated adjustments in one's social life. Even more tellingly, though we rarely stop to consider it, *life will eventually require us to relinquish every human relationship we hold dear,* whether as a result of growing apart, moving away, or as a consequence of the death of the other person or ourselves. Each of these necessary losses will carry its own unique pain, will have its own special poignancy. And yet, the only alternative to feeling the deep void associated with such losses is to lead shallow and noncommittal lives, in a sense forfeiting genuine attachments to people in an attempt to mitigate the pain of their inevitable loss. [2]

Because the inescapable transitions we undergo from childhood to old age diminish as well as enlarge us, it is important to recognize that all change involves loss, just as all loss requires change. My goal in this chapter will be to clarify some common features of the human response to major loss, examining both the immediate and longer range challenges it poses for those who experience it. Because grief resulting from the death of a loved one has received the greatest attention by scholars and researchers, we will first take a close look at some common processes of mourning, and how we can adapt to bereavement. Later chapters will explore some of the unique features of other losses, especially those stemming from the dissolution of relationships and the "symbolic" losses of jobs and social status brought about by other life changes.

All changes involve loss, just as all losses require change.

Anatomy of Grief

Much of what we know about the human response to loss derives from studies of adults who have lost a loved one through death. At least in these cases of profound and irretrievable loss, there appear to be certain common reactions, feelings, and processes of healing for those who are bereaved, although there are also important variations among mourners as a result of who they are, how they typically cope with adversity, and the nature of their relationship to the deceased individual. For this reason, it is misleading to speak of "stages" of grieving, as if all mourners follow the same path in their journey from painful separation to personal restoration. Thus, the discussion of the "typical" grief response that follows should be read as a rough sketch of general (but not universal) response patterns, and as a backdrop to the more detailed comments to follow on the contexts and meanings that affect grieving for particular mourners. [3]

For the sake of simplicity, the phases in a typical grief process will be presented as if they followed the sudden, unexpected death of a family member (as by an accident or fatal heart attack or stroke), with the recognition that this pattern may vary somewhat under other conditions, as when the death is the result of violence, trauma, or lengthy illness. Even in these cases, however, the mourner often encounters these common patterns, although their intensity or duration may vary from one loss to the next. Together, they form a "grief cycle" that begins with anticipation or learning of the death of the loved one, and that continues through a lifetime of adjustments that follow.[4]

Avoidance. Particularly in "high grief" deaths that violate our expectations for the continued life of the person we love, we may find the reality of the loss impossible to comprehend, and may respond initially with shock, numbness, panic, or confusion, in a sense muting or avoiding the full awareness of a reality too painful to absorb. Confronted by the harsh awareness of the death, we may react with, "Oh my God! It can't be true! There must be some mistake. I was just talking with him a few hours ago!" When circumstances regarding the death are ambiguous (as when a loved one is presumed dead in an airline disaster, but no body has been found), survivors can continue to hold on to the hope that their loved one has survived against all odds, until an admission of the bitter truth seems unavoidable. Even when the death is obvious and acknowledged at the outset, we find ourselves acting as if the person is still alive, perhaps by imagining that we see his or her face in a crowd, only to have our grief triggered again when we learn it is someone else. Yet as confusing as such experiences can be, they are normal reactions to loss, and reflect the difficulty we have in fully absorbing the news of a traumatic loss that leaves us irrevocably changed and diminished.

Physically, an individual in the avoidance phase may feel numb or "unreal," perceive the voices of others as far away, and in other respects feel distant or detached from his or her immediate surroundings. At a behavioral level, the survivor may appear disorganized and distracted, unable to perform even the routine activities of daily life, from making out a shopping list to paying bills. Thus, in addition to the emotional support that will be discussed later, at this phase grievers often can benefit from concrete help with the tasks required for continued living.

As fuller realization of the reality of the loss begins to sink in, vivid emotional reactions may begin to emerge, often including angry protests against those seen as responsible for the death—doctors, the drunk driver responsible for the accident, the deceased person himself, or even God. For many mourners, this tumult of feelings may be obvious to those around them, sometimes leading to misunderstanding and distancing when the bereaved person's irritability or resentment is directed at those seen as "more fortunate." For other grievers, the chaos of emotions that can emerge as avoidance erodes may be a private drama known only to them, as they try to carefully regulate the expression of their suffering in the presence of others. For most of us, the sharp awareness of public or private pain is punctuated by apparent denial of the reality of the death; one moment we behave as if the loss had not occurred, while an hour later we are overcome by grief and anguish. In a sense, orienting consistently to the reality of the loss would be like staring at the sun; it would be blinding if done too long. Instead, we typically begin to accommodate to the loss in degrees, glancing at it, and then away, until it becomes undeniably real, and its implications for our own future begin to be understood at an emotional level. [5]

---

s in a mall one day and thought I saw Cory walking ahead of me. It was a white-haired man is build, wearing a sport shirt like Cory always wore. It startled me for a moment... and I just had to walk closer to see his face, even though I felt like it was crazy.
—Bobbie, age 64

ien I was first asked to identify my brother's body after the accident, I just couldn't do it. His was bent way back, and his eyes were bulging.... I just couldn't see that body as Demetrius. It like I was in a cloud; everything was foggy, and I just felt numb, like nothing was real. And I kept feeling strange and separate like that for hours afterwards.
—Marcus, age 37

Assimilation. As we gradually absorb the full impact of the loss in the days and weeks that follow, we begin to ask, "How can I go on living without the person I love?" Unprotected by the shock and externalizing anger associated with avoidance, we begin to experience loneliness and sorrow in all of their intensity, learning the hard lessons of the loved one's absence in a thousand contexts of daily life. Twice a day, we set one less place at the table. Every night we sleep alone. We find ourselves having no one with whom to share a casual conversation about the events of the day upon returning home from work. We buy toys for someone else's child at Christmas after losing our own. When the deceased had suffered greatly prior to death, perhaps as a result of a long bout with cancer, our longing and grief may be moderated by relief, but may also be colored by guilt for having unconsciously "wished for" the loved one's death, as a way of mitigating his or her own pain, as well as our own exhaustion.

In the face of this deepening despair, we often constrict our activities and attention, withdrawing from the larger social world and devoting more and more attention to the compelling "grief work" that must be done to adjust to the loss. We may experience intrusive images or ruminations about the lost loved one, combined with nightmares of his or her death or dreams of the deceased person's return, only to find our unconscious hopes for reunion dashed against the hard realities of another day alone.[6] Depressive symptoms are a common accompaniment of this stage, including pervasive sadness, unpredictable crying spells, persistent disturbances of sleep and appetite, loss of motivation, inability to concentrate or take pleasure in work or play, and hopelessness about the future. Anxiety and feelings of unreality are not uncommon, extending to "hallucinatory" experiences of the loved one's presence.[7]

The prolonged stress characteristic of this phase also takes its toll on our physical health. Nervousness, choking sensations, nausea, and digestive disturbance are common, as are diffuse bodily complaints of pain that may come in "waves" lasting from several minutes to several hours. More ominously, unrelenting stress on the survivor's cardiovascular and immune systems can in extreme cases trigger heart failure or increase susceptibility to disease, accounting for the increased mortality of bereaved individuals in the year following their loss. Fortunately, however, most grievers ultimately overcome this physiological stress, as they gradually assimilate the reality of their loss and find ways of moving forward with their lives.

At first I was sure I was going crazy when I awoke in the night and saw my husband, who died, sitting at the edge of the bed and telling me, "everything will be all right." But being a

*l he was still there for me was strangely comforting, and other widowed friends have told me
they have had similar experiences.*

—Mary, age 66

*hen my wife died, I lost weight—a lot of weight. I just couldn't get myself to be interested in
nything, even eating. It's just like I lost the will to go on living. It took quite a while before I
started paying attention to my health again, and doing what was good for me.*

—George, age 42

Accommodation. Eventually, the anguish and arousal characteristic of
the assimilation phase begin to blend into a resigned acceptance of the reality of the death, as we start to ask, "What about my life now?" While yearning and loneliness persist for months or years beyond the death for most of
us, our concentration and functioning generally improve. Gradually, we reestablish a greater sense of emotional self-control and the return of normal
eating and sleeping habits. As in all phases of the grief cycle, progress is
never even, but typically comes in "two steps forward, one step back" fashion, with slow efforts at reorganization being punctuated by painful awareness of the loss that has been sustained.

As physiological symptoms of grief lessen, our energy returns in short
bursts, followed by longer periods of goal-directed activity. This allows us to
begin the long process of rebuilding the social world that has been shattered
by the loss, not by "replacing" the one who has died, but by recruiting and
strengthening a circle of relationships that are appropriate to the changed
life to which we must now adapt. Pangs of guilt and sadness may be felt
during this period, as the young widow explores new intimacies with men,
or a couple decides to "try again" following the stillbirth of a hoped-for child.
In many cases, this uneasy balancing act between remembering the past and
reinvesting in the future continues for the rest of our lives, requiring ongoing
readjustments that will be explored more fully in the next chapter. First,
however, it may be useful to examine briefly the typical course of adjustment
in the first two years following a death or other major loss, as a way of nor-

malizing the experience and allowing a more realistic anticipation of its duration.

———————

I know that there are some tangible things I need to do that I've been avoiding. I've been avoi...
it because it would really concentrate my emotions and bring them to the surface, and as long
was overwhelmed with grief, I was unwilling to do that.... I really need to say "good-bye" to .
father by visiting the boat he built. It symbolizes so much of his life, his dreams, his hopes, thi...
admired about him the most. It's much more "him" at this point than visiting the grave or ...
family home, which he also built. I've avoided it, and I know I need to do that. And I think
almost ready.

—Chris, age 42

———————

Levels of Functioning during Bereavement

How long is it normal to mourn the loss of a loved one? When this question was posed to a cross-section of Americans in a "man on the street" poll some years ago, the response was surprising: the overwhelming majority of those questioned gave answers ranging between 48 hours and two weeks. Clearly, these results convey the assumption that the impact of loss is temporary, and that the survivor will return to relatively normal levels of functioning within a matter or days or weeks. In contrast, scientific research on bereaved persons indicates that the actual course of grieving is far longer, with marked disruptions in the survivor's level of functioning persisting months following the loss, and subtler consequences reverberating throughout the rest of the bereaved person's life. To gain an overall sense of the ebb and flow of grief symptoms over time, a typical "recovery curve" following major loss is presented below, derived from research on a large group of adult mourners. [8]

friends expected me to be over the death of my son within a week, two weeks at the most, and a month was going a bit far. A lot of them said to me, "Aren't you over that yet?"
                                                                    —*Jim, age 32*

...en Ralph passed away, a lot of my friends just didn't understand. It's like they expected me to "just fine" within a week or so after the funeral! After a while I came to understand that they needed me to be "okay" because they just didn't know how to relate to me if I wasn't.
                                                                    —*Ruth, age 57*

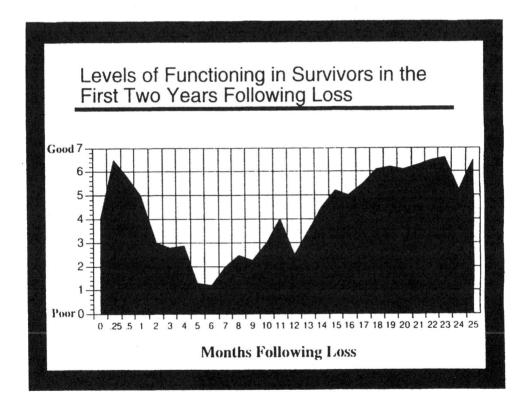

Levels of Functioning in Survivors in the First Two Years Following Loss

Months Following Loss

In the immediate aftermath of becoming aware of the loss, we typically experience extreme disorganization, at every level from our feelings (anguish, panic), to our thinking (disbelief, impaired concentration), to our behavior (agitation, sleep disruption). However, protected somewhat by the shock and numbness of the early avoidance phase, we often seem to "regroup" in the days that follow. During these earliest days of bereavement, we are also buoyed up by the intensive social support that often accompanies community awareness of the loss up to, during, and shortly after the funeral ceremony. It is during this period that other people are most likely to recognize our pain, and offer tangible assistance in the form of help with meal preparation, funeral-related tasks, and release time from work responsibilities.

Unfortunately, this apparent "recovery" is often fleeting, as we characteristically begin a long and uneven "slide" toward greater disorientation and depression in the weeks following the loss, "hitting bottom" only several months later. This period—beginning one to two weeks after the loss—coincides with our attempt to resume the demands of traditional roles at work and in the home, at the very time that social support by neighbors, employers, and relatives is withdrawn. If we do not have an understanding circle of confidants with whom we can "process" this confusing experience, the intensifying despair of this phase can become circular, with each uncontrolled emotional outburst or forgotten obligation being interpreted as further evidence that something is wrong with us or our way of coping. It is at this point that many bereaved persons reach out to clergy, doctors, counselors, or other professionals for help, given the growing gap between what others seem to expect of them, and what they feel able to muster on their own. The lack of ongoing rituals of support for the long period of readjustment complicates this process for many North Americans, leading too many bereaved persons to conclude that their continued distress is a sign of personal failure.

For me the real grieving didn't start until six months after the death. I was just numb up until that point, and then I realized, "It's Christmas and Eric is not here."
—Sally, age 37

With understanding and encouragement, however, we can be helped through these valleys of despair, to begin the long climb toward reorganization and renewal. Still, the path is a rocky one, with further deterioration in functioning to be expected on symbolically significant occasions (holidays, birthdays, anniversaries of the death), especially during the first year. Eventually, as we begin to integrate the lessons of loss and learn to cope with a world that is forever impoverished, the pain may be put into perspective, and life may be engaged more fully. But this process is a longer one than most people realize, unfolding over years rather than months, and involving periodic "grief spikes" years or even decades later. These experiences are a common and normal part of accommodating to the loss of someone (or something) precious to us, and should not be interpreted as some form of regression or lack of "resolution" of the grieving process.

---

me, the year after my husband's death was a year of "firsts": my first vacation taken without my first Christmas as a single mother, my first return to the workplace in many years. A lot of e were bittersweet, but some were really nice, like the first time I laughed aloud after he died, or e first time I realized I could do what I really wanted to, without having to get someone else's proval. There was a lot of pain in that first year or two, but as I look back on it now, there was also a lot of growth.

—Doris, age 45

---

one point I thought of grief as something time-limited, something that came when someone ied, but got "worked through" in a few months or years in most cases. Now I no longer think t way. My dad died when I was just a kid, but I've felt his absence keenly at many subsequent s in my personal development, like when I graduated from college without his being there to see ppen, or when my wife and I had our first son, who I realized would never know his grandfather. I don't think that the tears I cried at those times meant something was wrong with the way I had grieved, but more that my father continues to be an absent presence in my life, a part of who I am.

—Bob, age 39

Complicated Mourning

Although it is important not to "pathologize" grieving by presenting it as if it were an illness, it is also important to acknowledge that satisfactory reorganization of one's life following a major loss is not a guaranteed outcome. Indeed, there are several ways that we can become "stuck" in the grief cycle, so that grieving is apparently absent, becomes chronic, or is life-threatening. These negative outcomes may be more likely when the loss is a traumatic one (involving violation one's own body, as in rape or physical assault; or a loved one is victimized by violence or senseless killing, as by a drunk driver). "Off-time" deaths, which are "out of sync" with the family life cycle, also may be hard to accommodate, as in the death of a child that robs the parents and siblings of not only the child's present, but also expected future.[9] Characteristics of the mourner can also affect the process and outcome of bereavement, including reliance on maladaptive coping strategies, such as overuse of alcohol or anti-anxiety medication.[10] Finally, contextual factors (e.g., level of social support available to the mourner) can also promote or impede healthy grieving. One particularly tragic example of this is the phenomenon of "bereavement overload," in which an individual is confronted with the simultaneous or sequential deaths of so many significant others (e.g., in combat situations, or accidents in which several friends or family members are killed), that grieving each loss separately and fully becomes a near impossibility. In some communities, bereavement overload has become a way of life, as for gay men whose friends and lovers are dying excruciating deaths as a result of AIDS at such a rate that they may literally bury dozens of loved ones in a single year. Under such devastating conditions, it takes remarkable strength and mutual support to remain engaged with the living, while still honoring, loving, and caring for those who are dying.[11]

My wife and I had a child die 40 years ago when he was age 3. The death of Mary, our oldest at age 52, last year is just as difficult and I think even more so. It doesn't matter how old a child when death occurs.... It feels terribly wrong for your child to die before you.

—Jack, age 71

*Vhen I lost Michael last year, I felt horribly guilty because I just didn't feel the sadness that I
·ected to in losing someone I loved so much. But in the last few years, I've seen so many of my
·sest friends get sick and die from this terrible disease that I just feel shell shocked—like I can't
·ess one death before the next one comes. It's like something is frozen inside of me, and I'm not
sure what it will take to let it thaw.*

—Keith, age 43

How can you know when to seek help with your own grief experience,
beyond natural reaching out to your family and friends? One answer would
be to check whether you feel somehow "blocked" in your own grieving, unable to feel anything over a period of months for the loved one you have lost,
or conversely, whether you feel stuck in intense and unrelenting suffering, to
the point that your own well-being or that of those for whom you are responsible are in jeopardy. While it is not uncommon for a bereaved individual to wish that he or she could die, either to find release from unendur-
able suffering or to join the deceased in a better world, serious thoughts or
plans to end one's life call for professional consultation. At another level,
you yourself are probably the best gauge as to whether reaching out—to your
minister, your doctor, a support group, or a mental health professional—
could help you move forward with your own grieving and gradual reorganization. Though we must all attempt to find meaning in our losses and in our
continuing lives, there is no reason that we must do so heroically, without
the support, advice, and tangible assistance of others. We will return to this
process of personal and interpersonal meaning-making after considering some
of the other faces of loss, beginning with the loss of close relationships for
reasons other than death.

When should you reach out for help?

Although there is nothing "abnormal" about the pain, loneliness, and disruption that accompany bereavement, there are some conditions under which you may owe it to yourself and others to reach out to the professional or lay helpers in your environment: your doctor, minister, support group leader, or mental health professional. While the decision will be personal for each griever, you should seriously consider talking to someone about your grief symptoms if you experience any of the following conditions:

- *Substantial guilt,* about things other than the actions you took or did not take at the time of a loved one's death
- *Suicidal thoughts,* which go beyond a passive wish that you would be "better off dead" or could reunite with your loved one
- *Extreme hopelessness,* a sense that no matter how hard you try, you will never be able to recover a life worth living
- *Prolonged agitation or depression,* a feeling of being "keyed up" or "slowed down" that persists over a period of months
- *Physical symptoms,* such as stabbing chest pain or substantial weight loss, that could pose a threat to your physical well-being
- *Uncontrolled rage,* that estranges friends and loved ones or leaves you "plotting revenge" for your loss
- *Persistent functional impairment* in your ability to hold a job, or accomplish routine tasks required for daily living
- *Substance abuse,* relying heavily on drugs or alcohol to banish the pain of loss

While any of these conditions may be a temporary feature of normal bereavement, their continued presence is cause for concern and deserves attention by someone beyond the informal support figures in your life. Several such helping resources are listed at the end of this book.

pter 1 Research Notes

1. Forms of loss such as these that typically are given no formal cultural recognition are sometimes referred to as "disenfranchised," insofar as those who grieve for them are denied the support and status usually accorded to people mourning the death of a close relative. Occasionally, even those who have suffered conventionally recognized losses are disenfranchised in this sense, as when children, the mentally retarded, or frail older adults are assumed to lack the cognitive abilities to experience "grief" as it is usually understood. Unfortunately, this often results in the marginalization of whole classes of mourners, whose experiences may be misunderstood and disregarded by those around them.

While this is a useful concept, it is important to bear in mind that as social customs change, the boundaries that separate recognized from disenfranchised grievers undergo renegotiation. For example, many hospitals now offer psychosocial services for parents who have experienced the perinatal death of a child, allowing them to hold and name the baby, taking pictures of stillborn infants for parents who may later request them, giving parents receiving blankets to memorialize their wished-for child, and so on. Likewise, as this book is going to press, a number of large companies (including family-oriented enterprises like Walt Disney) are enacting more generous leave policies for bereaved employees who have lost unmarried partners (e.g., gay and lesbian or cohabiting partners). An intelligent discussion of unrecognized loss and its implication for grief theory is provided by Ken Doka (Ed.) (1989). *Disenfranchised grief.* Lexington, MA, Lexington Books.

2. An interesting extension of this idea considers virtually all forms of psychological distress as patterns of retreat from, or failure to engage in deep-going *role relationships*, in which we allow others intimate access to our most cherished and vulnerable perceptions, beliefs, and values. Significantly, a failure to invest in or risk genuine intimacies with others can represent an attempt to avoid the pain associated with their inevitable loss. The subtle movement toward or away from such relating can become a focus of psychotherapy, as discussed by Larry Leitner (1995), Optimal therapeutic distance. In R. A. Neimeyer & M. J. Mahoney (Eds.), *Constructivism in psychotherapy,*

(pp. 357-370). Washington: American Psychological Association. A some-what different treatment of this issue considers the avoidance of genuine re-lating to others as an expression of anxiety about our own eventual deaths and the losses these entail; see R. W. Firestone (1994), Psychological defenses against death anxiety. In R. Neimeyer (Ed.), *Death anxiety handbook* (pp. 217-241). Philadelphia: Taylor & Francis.

3. The presentation of typical grief responses that follows is intended to be descriptive only, in order to allow individuals who have suffered loss to place their own experience in a broader normative pattern. However, I share the reservations of many others about the implied prescriptiveness of such generalizations, and attempt to qualify and critique them in the pages that follow. This critique is sharpest in Part 2, where I provide the outline of an alternative understanding of mourning that contrasts in many ways with stage models.

4. This discussion parallels the more extensive presentation of phases of uncomplicated grief presented by Therese Rando's (1993) *Treatment of complicated mourning*. Champaign, IL: Research Press. Rando's work pro-vides an excellent clinical sourcebook for helping professionals, particularly in providing guidelines for treatment of psychosocial difficulties following bereavement. Although many other authors have advanced models of the typical emotional trajectory following a loss (some of which are cited in Part 2), the present description of the "grief cycle" represents my own distillation of prominent psychological responses to loss. My preference is for a simple three phase description, as elaborate multi-stage models risk making more assumptions about what is and is not a "normal" pattern of adjusting to the death of a loved one. The very general frame offered in this chapter will be expanded considerably as the book progresses.

5. The most recent research by Margaret Stroebe and her colleagues is based on a "dual process" model of mourning, which views accommodating to bereavement as requiring an ongoing shift back and forth between two contrasting modes of functioning. In the "loss orientation," the survivor engages in intensive "grief work," experiencing, exploring, and expressing

the range of feelings associated with loss in an attempt to grasp its signifi-cance for her or his life. At other times, in the "restoration orientation," the griever focuses on the many external adjustments required by the loss, con-centrating on work and home responsibilities, establishing and maintaining relationships, and so on, while "tuning out" the waves of acute grief that may come again. This model is useful in suggesting that some degree of "avoid-ance" of the reality of loss may be both helpful and common, and will be experienced throughout the adjustment process, rather than confined solely to its initial phases. My emphasis on avoidance as a first phase of the grief cycle simply acknowledges its predominance for many grievers in the first minutes, hours, and days following loss, and the greater attention to restora-tion of their lives that becomes more common later. For a discussion of the dual process model, including some of its implications for understanding differences in gender and cultural differences in grief behavior, see Margaret Stroebe, Henk Shut, and Wolfgang Stroebe (1998), Trauma and grief: A com-parative analysis. In J. Harvey (Ed.), *Perspectives on loss*. Philadelphia: Tay-lor and Francis.

6. These "intrusive" experiences (preoccupation, nightmares, flashbacks) are especially common and intense in cases of traumatic loss, representing the contrast pole of an intrusion-avoidance cycle. For a discussion of these issues in the context of post-traumatic stress, see Mardi Horowitz (1997), *Stress response syndromes* (3rd edition). Northvale, N.J.: Jason Aronson.

7. Once thought of as "pathological," reports of continued contact with a loved one who has died are now recognized as a common component of bereavement. For example, recent research indicates that 60% of bereaved individuals report experiences of sensing the presence of the deceased, with half of these describing it as a general, nonspecific awareness, while fewer, but still significant numbers describe visual, auditory, tactile, or even olfac-tory awareness of their loved one. Importantly, over 85% found such expe-riences comforting, while only 6% found them upsetting. (See Susan Datson & Samuel Marwit (1997), Personality constructs and perceived presence of deceased loved ones, *Death Studies, 21*, 131-146.) Results such as these call

into question traditional models of grieving as requiring detachment from the deceased, a theme that will be explored in more detail later in this book.

8. The research on which this description is based derived from a ten-year study of 1,200 mourners, which was informed by John Bowlby's and Colin Murray Parke's theories of bereavement as a process of separation from a lost love object, and the fluctuating and overlapping experiences of shock, yearning, disorientation, and reorganization that accompany it. I have simplified the prototypic graphs of each of these experiences in this brief discussion, and refer the interested reader to the original study for details. See Glen W. Davidson (1979), Hospice care for the dying. In H. Wass (Ed.), *Dying: Facing the facts* (pp. 158-181). Washington: Hemisphere.

9. Professional readers interested in a fuller discussion of grief and loss in the family context are encouraged to consult Froma Walsh and Monica McGoldrick (1991), *Living beyond loss*, New York: Norton, as well as Ester Shapiro (1994), *Grief as a family process*, New York: Guilford.

10. Of the "vulnerability factors" predisposing to intensified grieving, the most significant may be the previous level of adjustment displayed by the bereaved person. Thus, survivors who have been resilient in coping with other life challenges in adaptive ways are likely to cope similarly when faced with a major loss, while individuals whose previous adjustment was more fragile are more prone to intense and prolonged courses of grieving. For a recent study supporting this claim, see Louis A. Gamino, Kenneth W. Sewell and Larry W. Easterling (1998), Scott & White Grief Study (SWGS): An Empirical Test of Predictors of Intensified Mourning, *Death Studies*, in press.

11. For a sensitive and authoritative treatment of bereavement over-load in the gay community, see David Nord (1997), *Multiple AIDS-related loss*. Philadelphia: Taylor & Francis.

Chapter 2

To Love and to Lose

To this point, we have operated with an implied definition of "loss" in terms of bereavement, tacitly equating it with the loss of a loved one through that person's death. While intuitively appealing, a moment's reflection will persuade us that this is only the most obvious and publicly recognized form of loss, and that the experience of losing that which we love is ubiquitous in human life. Thus, it is important to adopt a broader frame, and define loss as any reduction is a person's resources, whether personal, material, or symbolic, to which the person is emotionally attached. [1] Although it would be impossible to address all types of loss that such a broad definition accommodates, it is critical to devote attention to two forms in particular because of their widespread and often repeated occurrence in our lives, and because of their impact on our psychological and social worlds. The first of these, relationship loss, is considered in this chapter, and the second, job loss, is taken up in the next.

While some aspects of the grief process outlined above may be most vivid when the loss occurs through death, other causes of separation can trigger many of the same reactions. For example, the loss of a marriage through divorce can throw us into a similar cycle of shock, anger, disorganization, and gradual reorganization on an emotional level. And as in mourning reactions associated with bereavement, we can become "stuck" in the grief that follows the loss of an intimate friend or lover with whom we have "broken up," finding it hard to imagine ever trusting or loving again. But other features of relationship loss are unique, particularly because it usually involves a complicated and emotionally-charged *choice* on the part of one or both partners to end a relationship that they once had mutually chosen to begin. For this reason it can be useful to focus on this distinctive form of loss before considering the ways in which we can move forward with our healing.

The Prevalence of Relationship Loss

When we stop to consider it, our experiences with loss, even in the best of circumstances, reach back into early childhood. Most of us can remember the sadness and confusion triggered by the death of a pet, even if the impact of this loss was minimized by the adults in our lives. Moreover, with each geographical move, or each "graduation" from one school to the next, we inevitably lose some friends while we gain others. Fortunately, for most children, the disorientation that accompanies these inevitabilities is brief and to some extent "invisible," with the losses usually being offset by the new opportunities for relating and learning that are opened up. For this reason, we often do not think of them as problematic, unless the child has more than the usual difficulty accepting the death of a pet hamster, or adjusting to the new environment. But in an important sense, the "practice" we receive as children in loving and losing is carried over into our later lives, shaping the way we cope with more mature losses. Under favorable circumstances, these early losses can help us develop resilience in the face of later challenges, and become secure in the knowledge that we and those around us have the resources to move through difficult experiences together. [2]

For many of us, the first vivid (and memorable) personal loss of our lives comes when we begin dating as adolescents. Our "first love," however superficial or fated for trouble it may seem in hindsight, was usually intensely meaningful at the time, often seeming like the center of our universe. Therefore it is not surprising when teenagers experience strong feelings of anger, guilt, or betrayal in the midst of breakups, sometimes to the point of becoming significantly depressed. The feelings of loneliness that accompany such losses are still harder to bear when parents and other adults minimize or dismiss the significance of these losses with simple reassurances that "there are other fish in the sea," or that "time heals all wounds." Instead, the adolescent needs to be treated as someone who is grieving, using guidelines that will be reviewed in Chapter 5 of this book.

—•—

hen Scott dumped me, my folks just kept saying, "Don't worry about it. Everything will be ight." But I wasn't allright. I was hurt and mad, and I didn't want them to take that away from me too.
                                                                        —*Jennifer, age 16*

—•—

Unfortunately, the loss of love relationships has become almost as commonplace in adult life as in the experimental years of adolescence. Data indicate that one in two lesbian couples, one in three gay partnerships, a similar percentage of heterosexual cohabiters, and one in seven heterosexual marriages will dissolve within two years. [3] To some extent, the instability in our elective relationships is inevitable, insofar as any relationship that is mutually chosen by two people can be "unchosen" by either of them. Moreover, such a pattern has its advantages, as experimenting with several possible close relationships in succession can contribute in its own way to our growth as people, with each relationship potentially adding something unique to the fund of experiences, perceptions, and shared histories that shape our personalities. But for many people, the years of dating represent a seemingly endless series of exhilarating romantic connections, broken by disappointing and occasionally devastating disconnections. In extreme cases, "shopping for a partner" can take the form of "addictive relating," an impatience in delaying gratification long enough to develop true intimacy with a partner, who is soon jettisoned in the process of pursuing the next conquest. When romantic partners are construed in this way as commodities to be consumed, the loss of the relationship *per se* might have fewer long term repercussions than the diminution in intimacy and meaning that this endless quest entails. [4]

In a sense, even the decision to affirm one romantic relationship as exclusive and permanent entails subtle corollary losses, in the form of missed opportunities to cultivate other possible relationships. In the excitement of early courtship the relinquishment of intimacy with others may be a distant concern, if it is considered at all. But as relationships cool and become more predictable, the lure of other relationships may grow, undermining our sense of satisfaction or commitment with our partners. [5]

Of the many forms of relationship loss, the most commonly studied is the dissolution of formal marriages through divorce. Indeed, statistics indicate that we Americans have become a divorcing people, with one half of all marriages begun in the last 10 to 20 years being destined for divorce. At one time, powerful social expectations bound spouses to one another "for better or worse, till death do them part." Now, however, all but the most conservative persons see divorce as a responsible way to solve marital problems, and the social stigma that once effectively prohibited separation is largely gone. Without condemning or condoning any individual's decision to end a committed relationship, it can be important to understand the causes, costs, and consequences of this choice. Even if we ourselves are not touched by relationship loss—at least prior to the death of our partner—the odds are high that at some point in their lives, many of our closest friends and family members will be.

The Trajectory of Relationship Loss

How does the ending of a relationship begin? At one level, the answer is different for every couple who separates. Sometimes the decision to separate is mutual and painfully negotiated across a period of years, and at other times it comes suddenly and "out of the blue" for the partner who feels "blind sided" by the decision of his or her spouse, who may have quietly contemplated the breakup for months or years. Usually it falls somewhere between these two extremes, as a growing sense of distance punctuated by angry complaints make both partners aware that "something has to change." Each of these paths toward dissolution has its own dynamic, and each has its own problems.

To understand the origins of the impulse to leave a close relationship, it is important to understand the source of the motive to enter it in the first place. None of us enters a committed relationship as a "blank slate," devoid of anticipations and expectations about what the relationship should be. Instead, we carry with us a fund of often unrecognized hopes and beliefs about what the "perfect spouse" should be, how roles and responsibilities will be distributed in the family, and how problems with one's partner should be solved. Moreover, we all have a "dream" of the ideal relationship, which includes (sometimes impossible) standards by which the partnership will be measured. This dream, shaped by our experiences in our families of origin, in previous romantic relationships, and by the general cultural messages contained in our folklore and media, almost inevitably fails to match the reality of life with our partner, whose own relationship belief system probably differs in major or minor respects from our own. While the loss of this dream can lead us toward mature renegotiation of the relationship with our partner, it can just as often plant the seeds of dissatisfaction that lead to the eventual abandonment of the relationship itself. [6]

Diane Vaughan has studied the reports of men women following separation and divorce, and has tried to identify a typical course of "uncoupling." Her interviews led her to distinguish between the initiator of the breakup and the one left behind, with the former unhappily ruminating about the state of the relationship and indirectly recruiting social support from others for the decision to leave long before that decision is announced to the partner. Typically, the "pulling away" is gradual, perhaps being more evident at a behavioral level (in terms of avoidance of sexual contact with the partner or "forgetting" to wear a wedding ring) than at the level of declared discontent. Meanwhile, the partner may be making conscious or unconscious attempts to ignore signals that something is wrong, instead persuading him- or herself and others that "everything is really okay." As the discontent of one or both partners becomes more evident, each tends to develop a different story or account of their difficulties, one that excuses the self and blames the partner for most of the difficulties in the relationship. Ultimately, however, both partners must grieve the loss of the relationship, though this grief may be tinged with guilt for the initiator, and with anger for the one who feels betrayed. [7]

————

I guess I knew for a long time that something was wrong in my marriage. Sally kept spend
more and more time away from me and the kids, and our checkbook just kept coming up sh
Looking back, there was plenty of evidence that she was thinking about leaving me, but I just
want to believe it. Eventually, I got angry enough that we just had it out, and then we both
that it was over.

—Ken, age 48

————

When couples separate, some of the costs are obvious, while others are more subtle. Certainly, the anger and frustration of one or both partners is usually evident to each, and their guardedness or impulsiveness about form-ing future relationships may be equally clear, at least to others who know them well. But other costs may be less expected. After a couple divides their possessions, a bedroom dresser without its matching chest of drawers may seem as lonely as its owner. The inevitable loss of income that comes with divorce can cost all family members recreational, personal, and perhaps edu-cational opportunities that might have been more feasible if the family had remained intact. And the usual necessity for one or both spouses to move after a divorce may cost them the familiarity and support of their neighbor-hood and circle of friends.

At a less tangible level, separation involves a loss of self-definition, just as does widowhood. No longer is one defined as part of a couple, as "belong-ing" to someone, but instead as an "independent" person, single again after perhaps many years of marriage. Not only does this transition require a major shift in one's view of oneself, as we shall see below, but it also is hard to assimilate for the people in one's social world. Complicating this transition still further is the fact that breaks are seldom "clean;" more often, they in-volve continued sporadic contact with one's ex-partner, sometimes to the point of emotionally complicated, but comfortingly familiar sexual reunions at points of loneliness for both. Moreover, the subtle costs of uncoupling are difficult to avoid even when the end of the relationship is hoped for, as one inevitably sifts through the ruins of the relationship in an effort to make sense of "what went wrong."

Finally, because many marriages end in the context of extramarital affairs, uncoupling may be accompanied by a deep sense of betrayal on the part of one spouse, and idealization of the new romantic partner on the part of the other. While "making a break" and seeking a new beginning elsewhere may indeed lead to greater eventual happiness for one or both spouses, this pattern can as easily contribute to a sense of suspicion on the part of the "abandoned" partner, and eventual disappointment with the realities of the new relationship on the part of the other.

Of course, the consequences of a separation are usually felt far beyond the partners themselves. When friends part ways, they tend to polarize others in their social circle as well. The respective parents of divorcing spouses often grieve the loss of relationships with members of the "other side" of the family, particularly when they had cultivated friendships with in-laws that are now strained by the estrangement of their children. And most tragically, children are often the greatest casualties of divorce, usually continuing to grieve the breakup of their parents' marriage well into their adult lives. Like adults in the assimilation phase of the grief cycle, children can angrily deny the reality or inevitability of their parents' divorce, cultivating the fantasy of eventual reunion or blaming themselves when it fails to materialize. We will return to the factors that promote healing of these and other loss-related wounds later, after briefly considering one final form of loss in adult life, namely, of status and security following the loss of one's occupational role.

ted it when Mom and Dad broke up, even though I was sick of the fighting. I hated the new tment, her new boyfriend, everything. And when they got married, it was like the end of the orld. I just held onto her at the wedding and cried and cried. I didn't want to let her go.

—Brian, age 12

Chapter 2 Research Notes

1. I have borrowed this definition from John Harvey and Ann Weber (1998), Why there must be a psychology of loss. In J. H. Harvey (Ed.), *Perspectives on loss: A sourcebook.* Philadelphia: Taylor & Francis. Readers interested in exploring the many faces of loss will find Harvey's work invaluable, especially because it draws upon experiences as diverse as illness, dissolution of close relationships, loss in sports, trauma, and homelessness. This same diversity is evident in the scholarly articles published in the journal he edits, entitled the *Journal of Personal and Interpersonal Loss* (see bibliography of suggested readings for details).

2. In the interests of space, I will not attempt adequate coverage of the unique features of children's grieving, or focus on special considerations in responding respectfully and sensitively to their needs in the wake of bereavement. For a comprehensive treatment of these issues, the reader may consult David Adams and Eleanor Deveau's (1995) book, *Beyond the innocence of childhood (vol. 3): Helping children and adolescents cope with death and bereavement.* Amityville, NY: Baywood, as well as Charles Corr and David Balk's (1996) *Handbook of adolescent death and bereavement.* New York: Springer. Other resources for dealing with bereaved children are listed in the resource directory at the end of this book. However, I will venture a few observations and suggestions relevant to children and families in Chapter 4, as well as in the chapters of Part 2.

3. See Susan Sprecher and Beverly Fehr (1998). The dissolution of close relationships. In J. H. Harvey (Ed.), *Perspectives on loss: A sourcebook.* Philadelphia: Taylor & Francis.

4. The despair that often accompanies the "singles scene" is explored by Gerald Alper (1994). *The singles scene: A psychoanalytic study of the breakdown of intimacy.* Bethesda, MD: International Scholars Publications. However, like many analysts, Alper tends to pathologize the people he studies, and disregard the potential viability of the single lifestyle as a way of organizing a substantial portion of our lives. While I have sometimes observed the

tendency among my psychotherapy clients to objectify others in the way the way Alper describes, by no means is this the exclusive prerogative of single people! Indeed, the tendency to treat one's partner as no more than an instrument for one's own gratification is all too prevalent in long-term "committed" relationships. Likewise, single people may simply be more judicious in committing to a partner than are those persons who marry impulsively or in response to social pressure. Thus, in this area, as in so many others, it is important to temper simple generalizations with the recognition that every statistical trend disguises considerable variability in individual cases.

5. Other outcomes are of course possible, of both a favorable and unfavorable kind. In ideal circumstances, partners continue to find their relationship mutually satisfying across the years, evolving as each member grows and changes. But this evolution tends to occur within bounds imposed by a core agreement on central values and ways of construing the world. In contrast, other relationships tend to lapse, especially when continued relating reveals deep-going incompatibilities between partners' values and constructions. For research on this dynamic in the context of the development and dissolution of friendships, see Robert Neimeyer, Donna Brooks and Kurt Baker (1996), Personal epistemologies and personal relationships, in D. Kalekin-Fishman and B. Walker (Eds.), *The construction of group realities*, Malabar, FL: Krieger.

6. This analysis of the role of beliefs and dreams in the dissolution of intimate relationships derives from Andrew Schwebel and Bryce Sullivan (1996), Coping with the loss of the marriage dream. *Journal of Personal and Interpersonal Loss, 1,* 57-70. They go on to illustrate how couples can adopt unconscious strategies, such as defensive avoidance and distraction by child rearing responsibilities, as a way of minimizing conflict and masking the extent to which the current relational reality falls short of the ideal.

7. For a detailed but readable account, see Diane Vaughan (1986), *Uncoupling: Turning points in intimate relationships.* New York: Oxford University Press.

Chapter 3

Job Loss and the Loss of Role

In an earlier day, many of us could rest assured in the knowledge that our life role, like our sex or race, was predictably determined. If our parents were farmers, well, then, farmers we would be. As occupations such as carpentry or homemaking passed from father to son and mother to daughter, there was a certain security in knowing "who we were" and what we would do, often for the rest of our lives. While the "foreclosed" quality of these decisions was sometimes stifling, it was nonetheless stable, ensuring a familiar plot to the story of our lives, even in the midst of other inevitable transitions.

With the coming of the industrial revolution and the advent of large, bureaucratic organizations, this pattern changed. One's life work was no longer pre-ordained or constrained to a small number of possibilities, but was instead determined by one's *choices* from among a seemingly limitless menu of options opened up by the increasing specialization of the work roles. But still, there was a certain predictability in *career paths* as individuals' work lives followed an "onward and upward" course through stable organization hierarchies.

This era of occupational stability is no more. With the shift from a modern industrial to a postmodern information based economy, many of the traditional large corporations are being destabilized by mergers, downsizing, reengineering, and outsourcing, effectively rendering the concept of "job security" obsolete. [1] At this point in our history, the average American will change not jobs, but *careers,* at least three times over the course of his or her life, each time requiring significant retraining for the new responsibilities entailed. Even when we ourselves seek such changes in our

work life, these months or years of occupational transition can be disorient-
ing, as we relinquish old patterns in pursuit of new potentials. But when job
loss comes unbidden (and often unexpectedly) as a result of a work-related
injury, layoff, or forced retirement, we can feel cheated, betrayed, and diminished by a loss that is not balanced by a compensatory gain. Because the loss
of occupational role confronts us with a number of unique stressors in addition to those that accompany other life transitions, we will consider these in
detail before discussing how people adapt to losses of all kinds, regardless of
their source.

I put in 28 years with that ad company, but when the new management was brought in, I wa
on the street in a matter of weeks. Now I don't know what I'm going to do. My wife went ba
work to make ends meet, but we can't even afford the house payments or the kid's tuition on
she can make on her own. And believe me, nobody wants to hire a washed up senior execut
when there are hundreds of young guys out there with better technical skills than I have who
willing and able to work for half the salary.

—Stan, age 56

The Role of Work in Life

When Sigmund Freud, the father of psychoanalysis, was once asked to
define the goals of a psychologically healthy life, his answer was simple: "To
love and to work." Yet while the central importance of loving relationships
and their loss is often clear to us, the centrality of work and work-related
losses is more easily missed. But in a real sense, we are what we do, and the
average American spends eight or more hours per day on the job, more time
than is spent in any other waking activity. Thus, it is hardly surprising that
we come to identify ourselves so closely with our work that "What do you
do?" is often the first question we ask a new acquaintance, and the first description we give when introducing ourselves to others.

Of course, our jobs provide more than just icebreakers for social interaction. They define many of our most significant life projects, giving us a sense of direction and purpose as we "work toward" a desired future. They reinforce our sense of self-confidence and self-esteem, as we earn paychecks, support ourselves and those we love, are granted merit raises, and receive recognition for superior performance. Even in a more humble, day-to-day sense, our jobs provide an organizing structure for our lives, and a social arena in which we interact with others as we exercise and increase our competencies. In this way our jobs define much of our past (what we have accomplished), our present (what we spend our time doing each day), and our future (what we are striving for), and to lose them is to shake the foundations of our identity and life plan.

Like other losses, job losses trigger familiar patterns of grieving. Anger and cynicism often accompany "being fired" from a position, particularly when the decision seemed merely bureaucratic or personally unfair. Moreover, because the targets of such anger are often safely removed from our rage and resentment, family members and close associates are likely to bear the brunt of our anger, leaving us further isolated in our pain. In fact, if not dealt with constructively, the powerful and insidious feelings triggered by being "let go" can combine with financial stressors to sabotage our close relationships as well, as reflected in the higher incidence of divorce and spouse abuse associated with recent unemployment.

The situation is hardly better when we suspect our layoff was "justified," and engage in a pattern of self-criticism and self-blame for "bringing it on ourselves." Indeed, in the cycle of searching for an explanation for our job loss, other people often explicitly or implicitly blame us for our "failure," compounding our shame and embarrassment. Moreover, the stigma of joblessness grows with the amount of time spent without work, particularly for traditional breadwinners. Thus, job loss must be understood not simply as a "stressful event," but as a *critical transition in the life course,* a process rather than a discrete event, and one that has an impact on our entire social network. [2]

Research has documented the pervasive effects of job loss on psychosocial functioning, as reflected in a decreased sense of competence and self-esteem, and increased levels of depression, anxiety, anger, and risk of interpersonal violence. As this cycle worsens, we may increasingly withdraw from others, and our situation can come to seem more and more hopeless. In the extreme case, the unemployed person can conclude that others would be "better off without him." When we have invested substantial parts of our identity in our work over a long period, the result can sometimes be tragic, as reflected in the fact that unemployed men over the age of 60 are at greater risk of suicide than any other demographic group. [3]

What makes job loss so difficult to endure? Among other factors, it places conflicting demands upon us that are not easily reconciled. On the one hand, like any other loss, job loss requires mourning, along with time to sift through the subtle and confusing feelings associated with this (desired or undesired) transition. On the other hand, unlike losses through death, there is no "ritual" that recognizes this loss or that provides a socially sanctioned period of grieving and recovery. If anything, social expectations run to the opposite extreme: we are expected to be relentlessly "self-motivated" and efficient in our pursuit of new work, at the very time that we feel most depressed, self-doubting, and unsure how to proceed. Faced with these conflicting emotional and practical demands, it is little wonder that we often procrastinate in our job search efforts, or retreat from the bruising rejections with which such efforts are met, all the while feeling more and more desperate about our future "salability."

In addition to these primary emotional challenges, the person who has lost a job faces a number of secondary social complications. The economic loss resulting from the absence of a paycheck can erode savings, and with it the resources to do things for one's family. As unemployment continues, it can result in a shift in the power dynamics in the family, sometimes undermining the previous breadwinner's authority and value in the eyes of immediate and more distant relatives. Thus, in some respects job loss may be even more difficult to accommodate than bereavement, per se, insofar as one's personal sense of desolation can be compounded with recrimination and diminished esteem on the part of oneself and others.

---

*'hen I lost the farm after the divorce from Sally, I knew I had to do something to earn a liveli-
d. I lived off of savings for nearly a year, always "planning" to start looking for work, but never
ly getting around to it. Everybody kept telling me I needed to "network" with people to get job
ads, but I just felt embarrassed when I approached them, like I was dependent on them for a
special favor or some kind of hand out. For a long time, I just couldn't face doing that.*

—Ken, age 48

These destabilizing effects of loss of life role are not limited to instances of release or retirement from gainful employment. For many older or middle-aged women who are widowed or left by husbands after long traditional marriages in which they worked in the home, the loss of the homemaker role can be at least as devastating. Faced—often unexpectedly—with the grief of relationship loss, they simultaneously lose their roles as wife, cook, family accountant, decorator, and social organizer that had been not only central to their own identity, but to the functioning of their family as well. Furthermore, they may feel helpless to pursue a successful job search, lacking the experience and skills needed to compete successfully with younger men and women who have more relevant backgrounds. Likewise, even when they can bring themselves to contemplate remarriage, they may find that their age or responsibility for dependent children can make finding a suitable partner difficult. Thus, to an even greater degree than career oriented men and women who lose their work roles, displaced homemakers can resign themselves to a financially and personally diminished existence from which they can envision no clear exit.

---

*'hen Harold left me for a younger woman I was stunned. How could he do that to me after I
ave him the best years of my life? I just felt like my life was over.... I didn't care about how I
ed, the shape of the house, nothing. It took a long time and a lot of support from friends before
I started feeling worthwhile again.*

—Connie, age 52

What is the process by which we negotiate such losses of people, relationships, and life roles? How do we move, however painfully, from a state of desolation toward a point of personal and social reintegration? How do we make sense of the losses in our pasts and find ways of moving forward toward a more desired future? In answer to these questions, we will consider the ways in which we attribute meaning to loss, and how we can accommodate to it in practical ways as we rebuild our lives.

pter 3 Research Notes

1. Mark Savikas discusses these shifts from an industrial to post-industrial economy and their implications for vocational behavior in his readable 1997 chapter, Constructivist career counseling: Models and methods. In G. J. Neimeyer & R. A. Neimeyer (Eds.), *Advances in personal construct psychology* (Vol. 4), pp. 149-182. Particularly interesting is his focus on three relatively recent developments in career counseling that are highly congruent with the meaning reconstruction approach introduced in later chapters of the present book: personal construct theory, biographical hermeneutics, and the narrative paradigm. Each in its own way construes individuals as managers of their own careers, and views meaning as deriving from the personal role of work in people's lives, rather than an objectively defined organizational culture.

2. This point is developed by Richard Price, Daniel Friedland, and Amiram Vinokur (1998), in Job loss: Hard times and reordered identity. In J. Harvey (Ed.), *Perspectives on loss: A sourcebook*. Philadelphia: Taylor & Francis. They go on to note how this transition is undergone differently as a function of the personal and social resources available to the unemployed person, both of an economic and psychosocial kind. In addition, their emphasis on the erosion of personal identity and sustaining assumptions (e.g., of self-control of one's destiny) are again congruent with a meaning reconstruction model of grieving, as considered in greater detail below.

3. The disconcerting link between job loss and suicidal behavior is vividly illustrated by the finding that fully one-third of all completed suicides are unemployed at the point of ending their lives (see Ronald Maris (1992), Overview of the study of suicide assessment and prediction. In R. Maris et al. (Eds.), *Assessment and prediction of suicide*. New York: Guilford). In view of this compelling correlation, it is remarkable that the psychological link between job loss and self-destructive behavior has been given relatively scant research attention, compared to the plethora of research studies on age, gender, marital, race, psychodynamic, and health-related correlates of suicide. When the relation of suicide to work has been studied systematically, it has

more commonly been from a relatively abstract sociological standpoint, tracing fluctuating suicide rates across "boom" and "bust" periods of economic activity, or comparing the rates for different occupations (see the chapter by Ira Wasserman entitled "Economy, work, occupation, and suicide" in the above cited volume for an example). Unfortunately, this inattention to the impact of loss is all too characteristic of the scientific literature, which has only recently begun to accord to loss the central role in research that it has long held in human life.

Chapter 4

The Activity of Grieving

hat matters is not what life does to you, but rather what you do with what life does to you.
Edgar Jackson

Almost by definition, bereavement is a "choiceless event." Few if any bereaved individuals would choose to lose those they love, just as few persons suffering other forms of major loss would invite what fate has dealt them. In this sense, at least, we are "victimized" by loss, the unwilling survivors of illnesses, tragedies, and misfortunes we would willingly have avoided had we been given a clear choice.

Ironically, perhaps, traditional understandings of grieving have perpetuated this sense of victimization. Stage theories of the emotional aftermath of loss are especially likely to depict bereaved individuals as essentially passive, thrust into an experience they must endure, but over which they have little or no control. At one level, this is true: we cannot simply "choose" not to be shocked, angered, or depressed by a loved one's death, or by the other major traumas in our lives. But as the philosopher Thomas Attig has pointed out, simplistic stage models of grieving are misleading in so far as they suggest that

> there is little choice of paths through the process. Rather the bereaved are thought to be assaulted by the event of death first, only to be swept along through ensuing events and experiences that unfold in an inevitable sequence and that are again choiceless. The process will run its course. Along the way, survivors will be sub-

jected to some combination of unwelcome, overwhelming emotion, physical exhaustion, intellectual confusion, spiritual crisis, and social upheaval. Given enough time and the capacity to endure, they will find themselves as some stage of reorientation, recovery, or the like. [1]

Among the unfortunate implications of this conception of mourning is the suggestion that there is little that bereaved individuals or those around them can do with or about their grieving. Instead, the person suffering loss must simply wait, on the assumption that "time heals all wounds." In sharp contrast to this position, Attig describes the grieving process as one that is rich in choice, with many possible paths or options to affirm or sidestep, approach or avoid. Central to this process is the task of "relearning the world," a world that has been forever changed by the loss. This chapter is about some of the choices and tasks with which loss confronts us, as we attempt to rebuild a life whose meaning is deepened by our continuing awareness of that which we no longer have, and our renewed appreciation for that which we do.

Although bereavement may be a choiceless event, the grieving experience understood as an coping process is permeated by choice.

Thomas Attig

Challenges of Mourning

In keeping with an understanding of grieving as an active process, grief therapists like William Worden and Therese Rando have outlined the "tasks" that must be accomplished by the bereaved individual in order to assimilate and transcend loss. [2] These have been reformulated and expanded here as a set of "challenges" to the mourner, which will be approached differently depending on the unique resources of a particular survivor and the distinctive nature of his or her loss. It is important to remember that these "tasks" are not to be accomplished in a particular order, nor are they ever "over and done with" in any final sense. Indeed, as we go through life, we will frequently have to relearn the lessons of loss in each new life context, just as the boy who grieves his father's death at age eleven must do so again in adulthood, perhaps when his own son reaches that age. Thus, the major losses that fill our lives pose ongoing challenges, to which we must return again and again at later stages of life's journey. With this recognition in mind, it is useful to spell out these challenges in more detail, from the most obvious of tasks facing the newly bereaved individual, to the most subtle of those that present themselves at later points in the "grief work" process.

Acknowledge the reality of the loss. While this task may seem obvious, the challenge it presents to us can be a complicated one. What is required is learning the lessons of loss at a deeply emotional level, through a series of seemingly unending confrontations with the limitations posed by our injury, the loved one's absence, or the unavailability of a valued role that once helped define our sense of self. Achieving a sense of "closure" regarding this task is especially difficult when our loved one is "physically present but psychologically absent," as in the case of a parent or spouse's increasing dementia as a result of Alzheimer's disease, or when he or she is "psychologically present but physically absent," as in the case of MIA's or abducted children. In such instances, giving up hope for a cure or reunion can feel like abandonment of the loved one, and can be all the more problematic when family members are divided among themselves about the realistic prospects for the other's restoration.

Acknowledging the reality of the loss has a second dimension as well, because we grieve not merely as individuals but as members of larger family systems. This suggests that acknowledgment and discussion of the loss needs to occur among all those who are affected by it, taking special care to include children, the ill, and elderly in family conversations. [3] In the case of the death of a family member, children in particular are at risk of being marginalized through misguided attempts to "protect" them. Euphemizing the loss ("Jesus took your little sister to heaven because he wanted a beautiful flower for his garden") not only mystifies the reality that the child may be struggling to understand, but also implies that the child's grief and loss are somehow inappropriate and not open to discussion. Similar cautions apply in cases of divorce. In the place of "protecting" the child from these harsh realities, it is more helpful to initiate discussions about how bereaved children are feeling, to physically comfort them, and to provide reassurance that they are still loved and will be cared for. Children's questions should be answered in a straightforward, direct fashion, and in terms of the family's shared beliefs regarding family roles, separation, death or the afterlife. A useful rule of thumb is that *if children are old enough to formulate questions about these losses, they are old enough to deserve appropriate answers.* While it is important to adapt our mode of communicating about the loss to the level of understanding of the listener, excluding anyone from the circle of open discussion risks isolating that person in his or her grief, and complicating later adaptation.

Open yourself to the pain. In the immediate aftermath of learning of a loss, numbing or distancing from the excruciating pain is to be expected. However, an ongoing attempt to mitigate or avoid the more distressing feelings triggered by the loss may delay or perpetuate grieving. In private moments of reflection and contemplation, or in shared moments of intimate discussion, bereaved persons typically need to sort through and identify the nuances of feeling that require attention. Does a pang of deep loneliness indicate the need to reach out and hold others you love? Does a wave of anxiety suggest the need to seek solace in prayer? Does a fit of self-condemnation signal the need to rationally review your efforts and accept your fallibility as a human being? Without a willingness to embrace the pain long enough to harvest its lessons, we tend to proceed through the loss blindly, trying to orient to the demands of external reality without an internal compass. Developing a delicate awareness of our emotional lives lets us negotiate the remaining challenges of our grief work with a sense of direction, cultivating a personal depth and wisdom as we do so.

On the other hand, focusing relentlessly on the pain of loss can be a bit like staring unblinking at the sun—it may actually be damaging if our gaze is sustained too long. For this reason, contemporary grief theorists have begun to emphasize that mourning typically involves periodic "grief work"—attending to one's internal feelings of sadness, desolation, anxiety, reflecting on the deceased, reviewing photographs—and reorientation to the practical tasks of home and work that not only must be attended to in their own right, but also give needed respite from the anguish of active grieving. Moreover, this latter, more "outward" focus is more than just "treading water," as it may include the development of a host of new competencies required to cope with a changed environment. Thus, grieving typically involves a process of fluctuating between *feeling* and *doing*, in different ratios depending on the individual griever and the relationship that has been lost. From this perspective, grieving only becomes complicated if one engages in one orientation to the exclusion of the other, in effect getting "stuck" in relentless rumination or prolonged avoidance of the pain. Bereaved individuals therefore need to give themselves permission to both immerse themselves in their grief, and to distract themselves from it as the practical or psychological need arises.[4]

--- · ---

...hout a willingness to embrace the pain long enough to harvest its lessons, we tend to proceed ...ugh the loss blindly, trying to orient to the demands of external reality without an internal compass.

--- · ---

Revise your assumptive world. The experience of major loss not only robs us of our possessions, capacities, or loved ones, but it also frequently undercuts the unspoken beliefs and assumptions that previously had been the building blocks of our philosophy of life. A crippling accident destroys our feeling of invulnerability. The special tragedy of a child's death violates our sense of justice, or perhaps even our belief in a just God. A robbery strips us forever of the feeling of safety that had been taken as a "given" until the break-in. Because the fundamental revisions required by the invalidation of our assumptive world can carry far-reaching implications for our behaviors, commitments, and values, they frequently require considerable time and effort, and continue long after the reality of the loss itself has been assimilated.[5]

Faced with a world that appears random, unfair, or even malevolent, we can respond in any of a number of ways, ways that ultimately dictate how we and those around us will accommodate to the loss. On the one hand, we can engage in self-recrimination, blaming ourselves for not foreseeing and preventing the loss, even when others would not hold us accountable. Thus, the department head who is "let go" when his hospital "downsizes" may endlessly criticize himself for not seeing it coming and transferring to another area or facility before he is pushed unexpectedly into an uncertain entrepreneurial future as a "consultant." Similarly, the young mother whose infant daughter dies of crib death may experience profound and lasting grief tinged with guilt, imagining that her child might still be alive if only she had been there at the right moment. The depressive self-criticism characteristic of such cases may appear circular and self-defeating, but at some level may be easier to accept than the complete abandonment of the cherished assumption that we can control the most important aspects of our lives.

On the other hand, it is also possible to respond to loss, even traumatic loss, by reaching out to supportive others, and in the process remind ourselves that the world is not wholly malevolent. Even more fundamentally, we can view the loss as a "wake up call" to review our sense of priorities, and ensure that we are giving our time and attention to those people and projects that are most precious, in view of our finitude as human beings. On review, we may find that some of the assumptions undercut by our loss were illusions that served as a cocoon against the reality of human contingency and frailty, beguiling us with the false sense that there "is always plenty of time later" to attend to that which is important, while we fritter away valuable hours, weeks, and years on superficial relationships and concerns, ultimately leading shallower and more noncommittal lives as a consequence. By incorporating the reality of the trauma into our revised assumptive world and assigning it a personal meaning, we may be transformed by tragedy, and made "sadder but wiser" by the experience. [6]

I used to think that if you did all the right things everything would work out right. You know *your parents, meet the right guy, have a story book marriage and three children and live h* *ever after. Then one day your child gets sick and dies, and you think, "It's not fair!" and t.* *where the anger comes in. It's not supposed to happen that way, but it does.*

—Janet, age 42

Reconstruct your relationship to that which has been lost. Particularly in cases of the death of loved ones or the dissolution of relationships, bereaved individuals can feel compelled to "forget" the one they have lost, in a mistaken belief that they must "move ahead without looking back." In fact, older grief theories often stressed the importance of "withdrawing emotional energy" from the relationship to the deceased in order to allow one to "reinvest" in new relationships. Such models seem to assume that love is like money, a fixed sum that must be withdrawn from one investment in order to be spent elsewhere.

Contemporary research on bereaved individuals teaches a different lesson. According to Stephen Shuchter and Sidney Zisook, the majority of widows and widowers report that they continue to sense the presence of the deceased spouse over one year following the death, and a substantial minority reported "talking" to the spouse regularly. Moreover, for the vast majority of these survivors, this presence is experienced as comforting rather than upsetting, encouraging the survivor to do what is necessary in his or her own life rather than remain fixated on the past. [7] Similar findings are reported Susan Datson and Samuel Marwitt, who discovered that 60% of individuals who had lost a loved one within the last two years had experienced the perception of their presence. For half of these persons, the sensed presence was of a general, nonspecific sort, such as feeling their loved one standing near the foot of their bed. However, nearly 20% reported hearing or seeing their lost loved ones, and 10% and 4% respectively reported feeling or smelling them. Of these "perceivers," approximately 80% found the experience comforting and maintained that they would welcome more such "contact" in the future. Although there was a tendency for perceivers to score higher on a test of "neuroticism" than nonperceivers, reflecting their somewhat higher levels of anxiety and distress, in general the frequency and function of the perceived presence of the deceased suggested that it was a relatively common part of normal bereavement, rather than representing a psychotic or pathological sign, as older grief theories might suggest. [8]

In view of such findings, it is perhaps more accurate to say that death transforms relationships, rather than ending them. What seems necessary is not so much distancing from memories of the loved one, but embracing them, and changing the relationship from one based on physical presence to sym-

bolic connection. This continued tie to the memory of the other is sometimes reaffirmed through a cherished "linking object," such as a well-worn
sweater of the father who is gone, or a favorite toy of a toddler who has died.
The preservation of connection to a vital relationship in the past can give
continuity to a life story disrupted by loss, as the survivor undertakes the
hard work of inventing a meaningful future. [9]

Other forms of relationship loss, such as divorce, require the mainte-
nance of a "real life" link with our estranged partner. Particularly in the case
of families with children, ex-partners need to find cooperative rather than
conflictual ways of continuing parenting tasks, and strive to prevent this from
being sabotaged by lingering resentments. Even in "childless" relationships
in which one partner leaves the other, it is often helpful to pack up and store
memorabilia about the relationship (photos, gifts, etc.), rather than discard
them immediately. Putting away these sentimental mementos of a time together can lessen the pain of being surrounded by constant reminders, while
still permitting one to sort through them at a future occasion when one's
"grief work" requires new perspective taking.

Reinvent yourself. In a very real sense, a part of us dies each time we
lose someone we love. Because we are social beings who literally construct
our identities in relation to the significant people in our lives—parents, partners, children, friends—the loss of these people creates a void in us as well.
Never again will that special person who shared an important part of our
past be there to call out that shared fund of memories and experiences tied
uniquely to that relationship. Even in less "final" forms of loss, such as moving to a new city or taking a new job, the loss of one's familiar surround can
destabilize one's sense of self, just as it requires the establishment of new
relationships. Whether we like it or not, we will never be our "old self again"
following a major loss, although with effort, we can rebuild an identity appropriate to our new role, while establishing continuity with the old.

Tom Attig eloquently develops this notion of identity as a social, rather
than exclusively personal phenomenon in his metaphor of a web of connectedness, which links us with those persons, activities, and places in which we
invest our caring. [10] In this image, death and loss tear the vital strands of
connection that define who we are, and we only effortfully and gradually

repair them by reestablishing other forms of connection to that which we had lost, as well as to the new world into which we are thrust.

———

All that which has touched and shaped us is with us still.

———

The need to reinvent oneself is also closely connected with the revision of one's assumptive world. As we sift through the lessons of loss, we can come to approach life with renewed priorities, with a clearer sense of what is important, and what is not worthy of concern. As we revise the philosophies by which we live, we also "re-vision" ourselves, perhaps opening ourselves to possibilities that once seemed foreclosed, developing skills and interests that previously have lain dormant within us, or cultivating relationships with others that previously had been neglected or unexplored. In this sense, while loss diminishes us, it can also lead to our renewal. Although the loss of familiar forms, work roles, and relationships can be unsettling and even threatening, it also can challenge us to enlarge our identities and integrate the hard-won wisdom that comes with survivorship.

———

ther we like it or not, we will never be our "old self again" following a major loss, although we can rebuild an identity appropriate to our new role.

———

If one squarely confronts the challenges of grieving, accepting with serenity those things that cannot be changed, and having the courage to change the things one can, what can one realistically expect as an outcome of the grief process? Again, psychological research suggests some hopeful answers. Although the great majority of widowed persons studied by Schuchter and

Zisook still feel a year after their loss that "a part of them is missing," virtually all also report that their lives "have great richness," and that they "try to get the most out of each day." While it may be difficult to believe in the midst of protest or despair that we will ever be able to adapt to a profound loss, survival, adaptation—and yes, even growth—are indeed possible. In a deep sense, the pain of loss is a mirror that reflects the preciousness of the attachments that sustain us, and the frailty of life can provide a necessary reminder of the need to ground one's living in ultimate concerns.

God, grant me the serenity to accept the things I cannot change, The courage to change the th can, And the wisdom to know the difference.

Reinhold Niebuhr

ipter 4 Research Notes

1. Attig makes this point in his 1991 article entitled "The importance of conceiving of grief as an active process," *Death Studies, 15*, 385-393. In contrast to the essential passivity of grieving in traditional models, some contemporary theorists view it as a process that involves an effortful attempt to reacclimate oneself to a world in which a central person, place, or project has been lost. In the present chapter I concentrate on models of mourning that emphasize cognitive and emotional tasks confronted by the griever. These models represent an advance over more stagic conceptions of grieving, in so far as they go some distance toward seeing the bereaved individual as an active agent struggling to adapt to a transformed life. In Part 2, however, I acknowledge the limitations of this conception, and present the framework of an alternative conception of grieving as a process of *meaning reconstruction*, a theme which will be foreshadowed in the remaining chapters of Part 1.

2. See for example Worden's (1996) book, *Children and grief*, New York: Guilford; and Rando's (1993) *Treatment of complicated mourning*, Champaign, IL: Research Press. Worden sees the bereaved child or adult as confronting four tasks that must be to some extent resolved as part of the individual's overall adaptation to loss, although these do not present themselves in any fixed order, and each may be revisited from time to time. The tasks include (1) accept the reality of the loss, (2) experience the pain of the loss, (3) adjust to an environment in which the deceased is missing, and (4) relocate the dead person within one's life and find ways to memorialize the dead person. Rando's conceptualization is somewhat more elaborate, consisting of six "R processes" of mourning, each of which entails various subprocesses. The major processes include: (1) recognize the loss, (2) react to the separation, (3) recollect the deceased and the relationship, (4) relinquish old attachments to the deceased and the old assumptive world, (5) readjust to move adaptively into the new world without forgetting the old, and (6) reinvest in new relationships and pursuits. Rando further distinguishes her "processes" from Worden's "tasks" because of necessary overlap among them and the nonlinear movement of the deceased individual through them over time. Both models are clinically useful, and superior to traditional stagic alternatives in

recognizing the complexity of actual grieving, and what might be done to facilitate it.

3. This injunction is extended by Froma Walsh and Monica McGoldrick (1991), *Living beyond loss*, New York: Norton. They explicitly borrow Worden's task model of grieving, but construe the tasks as applying to families rather than individuals per se. In addition, they offer an extremely useful discussion of the impact of loss as a function of the stage of the family life cycle at which it happens. For example, the death of the mother in a family poses quite different adaptational tasks for surviving family members if her children are five and seven years old, as opposed to twenty-five and twenty-seven. Traditional models tend to neglect both the family context and these developmental considerations in construing grief as a uniform process.

4. This "dual process" model of grieving is developed most systematically by Margaret Stroebe and her colleagues, based on their research in not only Western cultures, but also non-Western societies in which the norms of grieving are quite different. Theoretically, they distinguish between a "loss orientation" in which bereaved individuals do the emotionally taxing "grief work" associated with making sense of their loss, and a "restoration orientation" in which they deal in practical ways with the many secondary changes in their lives and roles occasioned by their primary loss. Oscillation between these two foci is normal, in their view, and does not represent some stage-like progression toward recovery, or some form of regression in the face of renewed pain after a "successful" period of coping with external demands. See Margaret Stroebe, Henk Schut and Wolfgang Stroebe (1998), Trauma and grief: A comparative analysis. In J. H. Harvey (Ed.), *Perspectives on loss: A sourcebook*. Philadelphia: Taylor & Francis.

5. This point is developed eloquently by Ronnie Janoff-Bulman and Michael Berg in their 1998 chapter, "Disillusionment and the creation of value," in J. Harvey (Ed.), *Perspectives on loss: A sourcebook*. Philadelphia: Taylor & Francis. Like other constructivist theorists (see Part 2), they view people—even very young children—as constructing high-level generalizations about the self and others. By adulthood, these generalizations ("I will

be taken care of," "The world is predictable") function as "our most abstract, general schemas, residing at the very foundation of our cognitive-emotional systems. Here they are typically insulated from direct behavioral challenges, which are more apt to address our narrower, more specific assumptions about ourselves and our environment." However, basic losses—especially of a traumatic kind—can cruelly put the lie to these taken-for-granted foundations, and force massive revisions of our outlook toward life, for better or worse. For a detailed clinical illustration of this process in the context of therapy for post-traumatic stress disorder, see Robert Neimeyer and Alan Stewart (1996), Trauma, healing, and the narrative emplotment of loss. *Families in Society, 77*, 360-375.

6. In drawing attention to the transformative process that can be set in motion by loss, Janoff-Bulman and her colleagues echo existential philosophers and psychotherapists, who argue that the stark and anxiety-producing confrontation with the reality of our eventual mortality is a precondition to living more authentically in the present. For an elaboration of this view in the context of death education and psychotherapy, see W. G. Warren (1989), *Death education and research: Critical perspectives*. New York: Haworth; and Robert Firestone (1994), Psychological defenses against death anxiety. In R. A, Neimeyer (Ed.), *Death anxiety handbook*. Philadelphia: Taylor & Francis. This theme of the rebuilding of the assumptive world figures prominently in the meaning reconstruction model that is detailed and illustrated in Part 2.

7. See S. R. Shuchter and S. Zisook (1993), The course of normal grief. In M. Stroebe, W. Stroebe and R. O. Hansson(Eds.), *Handbook of bereavement: Theory, research, and intervention* (pp. 23-43). New York: Cambridge University Press.

8. See Susan L. Datson and Samuel J. Marwitt (1997). Personality constructs and perceived presence of deceased loved ones, *Death Studies, 21*, 131-146. They also found that perceivers and nonperceivers did not differ on such demographic factors as gender, income, and religious affiliation, and that both groups reported equally adequate levels of social support. Finally, perceivers tended to be more extroverted than nonperceivers, an unexpected

finding that further argues against an image of these survivors as somehow more reclusive and disconnected from living relationships than their counterparts without the experience.

9. Some of the best contemporary thinking on the preservation of a connection with the "internal representation" of the deceased has been contributed by Dennis Klass, based on his intensive qualitative research on parents who have lost children. For his most recent work on this topic, see his 1997 article, The deceased child in the psychic and social worlds of bereaved parents during the resolution of grief. *Death Studies, 21,* 147-176.

10. Attig's 1996 book is entitled *How we grieve: Relearning the world,* New York: Oxford University Press. To a greater extent than other kindred spirits like Klass, Attig focuses on the practical as well as cognitive adjustments required of the bereaved person, and grounds his discussion in moving accounts of individuals who have suffered various kinds of loss. For this reason, it is accessible to both lay and professional readers. It is also highly compatible with the perspective developed in Part 2 of this book.

Chapter 5

Context and Connection

All too often, mourning is described as if it were a strictly individual process, as if each of us were an island buffetted by the waves of misfortune, unconnected to anyone or anything beyond ourselves. While loss does indeed have deeply personal meanings, and we must respect our need to do some of our "grief work" privately, it is worth reminding ourselves that much of this grief work has to do with affirming, strengthening, and enlarging our connectedness to others. In this chapter we will highlight the central place of relating to others in the context of our loss, both from the standpoint of what others can offer us through the gift of their caring, and what we can offer them in return.

ng Our Story

We live our lives as stories. Like novels, our lives have original beginnings, middles, and ends. They have a distinctive "plot" structure, a meaningful sequence of events that reveal who we are and shape who we become. They include a varied cast of characters interacting across time in scenes both tragic and comic. And they can be segmented into chapters that correspond to the major "periods" of our lives, whose titles and organization would vary depending on the life they describe (The Innocence of Youth, Childhood's End, Coming of Age, etc.). [1]

When we experience a major loss, the expected development of this life story is disrupted. Like a novel that loses one of its major characters halfway through the book, future chapters must somehow be rewritten to both account for the loss in a coherent way, and allow the plot to move forward with those that remain, perhaps introducing new characters along the way. The revised plot may reestablish the identity, strength or perseverance of the central character, or may depict the unanticipated growth of the "hero" as he or she rises to the occasion.

How do we go about reestablishing the plot structure of a life that has been disrupted by trauma or loss? We do so by telling and retelling our story in the context of listeners who care, each of whom contributes, in a unique way, to the further evolution of the narrative. As the psychologist John Harvey notes, "as people share their stories with others, they name and shape the meanings of their unique life experience." [2] Our stories are ways of putting in order a confusing series of events, finding underlying themes that tie them together and make them, if not acceptable, at least comprehensible. In our private construction of the story of our adversities, we attempt to answer the questions, "Why did this happen?" and "What could this mean?" In the public telling of our tales we seek help in finding answers, or at least permission to share the burning questions. Although no one can provide a prepackaged plot that answers these questions and charts our personal future, they can suggest themes, secular or spiritual, that we can use to weave through the events we are seeking to understand, and in the listening, let us grope toward a new sense of coherence.

I didn't want people to say things to me or give me advice. I just wanted them to listen to r wanted to talk and talk and pour it all out.

—Herb, age 52

Research suggests that the ability to share our feelings and stories of loss with others is indeed healing. Survivors of trauma who are able to confide in others about their experience show improved psychological and physical health, have fewer doctor's appointments, fewer signs of stress, and report feeling less depressed and overwhelmed by the misfortune they have suffered. And yet, hearing our story of loss and suffering may be difficult for listeners, requiring us to understand them as persons in their own right, with their own unique set of strengths, limitations, and sensitivities. To gain a clearer appreciation of the possible perspective of others, it is helpful to place the experience of grief in the family context, understanding more deeply its impact on different members of the family system.

----

people share their stories with others, they name and shape the meanings of their unique life experience.
—John Harvey

Family Crucible

Almost by definition, grief tends to be an isolating experience. We may feel preoccupied with our own pain, and find it hard to believe that others are suffering as intensely as we are. When we have lost someone or something dear to us, we may tend to discount the anguish of others "once removed" from the loss. We may minimize the suffering of a brother or friend of the deceased, when we have lost a husband. Even when we recognize at one level that others are attempting to grapple with the meanings of this shared loss in their own ways, we may gloss over a self-evident, but all-too-elusive truth, that *those to whom we most need to turn for support in our own grieving have also been wounded by the same loss.* Ironically, then, we find ourselves reaching out for support to those who may feel most incapacitated to provide it.

Does this mean that we should try to contain our own grief, so as not to "burden" others with our pain? Not at all. A corollary of the above truth is that, despite our woundedness, we are also the most relevant persons to offer support to those who have suffered directly or indirectly as a result of the same loss. As long as we do not seek—or offer—"easy" answers to the hard questions that constitute our mourning or that of others, we can share the burden of loss with those we love, and in so doing, make the burden a little less heavy.

If we are to share our grief work with significant others, we need to be aware of and respect their own "styles of mourning." No two people adapt to loss in the same way, and except in the broadest outlines, there is no "correct" way to grieve. This message may be especially difficult to assimilate when we are confronted with family members whose style of mourning is very different from our own—the adolescent who spends more time in her room, the man who throws himself into his work, the woman who cries unpredictably in public places. When the manner of experiencing and expressing grief differs among family members, it may require special sensitivity to find ways to "join" others in their own style of grieving, and create an atmosphere of understanding in which each person can speak of his or her unique struggle in his or her own words.

It is important to realize that those to whom we most need to turn for support in our own grief have also been wounded by the same loss.

Gender Differences in Grieving

Here, as in many other areas of life, research has suggested that sex differences must be understood and respected, even as partners try to find a way of talking with one another across the divide. "Women's grief" is more clearly understood, as widows have been the subject of much more research than have widowers. In fact, it is likely that the tendency of grief theorists to focus on the *emotional* aspects of grief work, sometimes to the exclusion of cognitive or behavioral modes of adapting, may reflect the greater vividness of emotions for the women who constitute the subjects of their studies. In contrast, men may be more likely to cope with the loss intellectually or philosophically, or by immersing themselves in the million-and-one instrumental tasks that confront survivors when a death occurs—funeral arrangements, death notifications, negotiations with insurance companies, and so on. Whereas women in crisis may naturally turn to others to give and receive support and openly express their feelings, men may feel the need to be more stoic, reporting a tendency to "push feelings away" in order to be "strong" for others.

Although these gender differences may be real, it is important to recognize that they are only depictions of typical male and female mourning styles in Western culture, and that any actual individual may grieve differently than these "average reactions" suggest. For this reason, Terry Martin and Ken Doka focus less on the grief responses of men and women, than they do on "feminine grief" and "masculine grief," explicitly recognizing that many females may resort to intellectualization, anger, guilt about not having succeeded in "protecting" the lost loved one, and assertion of self-reliance—all stereotypically masculine ways of dealing with grief. Likewise, many men will feel comfortable mourning in a more feminine style, sharing intense feelings and self-doubts with a circle of friends, or seeking help with especially troublesome dimensions of loss in a support group. [3] Thus, it is critical to understand the ways in which each of us as individuals grieves in accord with, or differently from, the "norm" for our gender.

While many of these gender differences are simply to be honored, rather than criticized as signs of "weakness" in women or "lack of caring" in men, some sex differences are more ominous. For example, Schuchter and Zisook found that more men than women reported high levels of alcohol consumption a year or more after bereavement, as well as a continued difficulty in "accepting" the finality of the loss. When these findings are considered in relation to the fact that men are over twice as likely to be involved in a new romantic relationship within the first year after the death of a spouse, they suggest that men may be at greater risk for trying to suppress and move beyond the pain of loss, rather than face it squarely. Thus, it is not surprising that more women than men report good to excellent adjustment in the second year following loss, although a significant minority may continue to feel somewhat "helpless" in their widowhood. [4]

Despite these differences, it is clear that men and women are more similar than different in their grief processes. For example, Schucter and Zisook found that the majority of both sexes report continued feelings of yearning for the deceased spouse a year following the loss, and similar numbers of men and women say they cry when thinking about their partner. It is often the *ways* in which males and females seek support that distinguish them, rather than their need for support, *per se*. For instance, parents who have suffered the death of a child are typically both profoundly affected by the loss, but they may reach out to one another in the crisis in different ways. Not uncommonly, the wife may want to discuss the child's death with her husband, only to feel rebuffed by his quickly changing the topic. Husbands, on the other hand, may reach out to their wives sexually, only to have their implicit bid for physical comforting rejected as "unbelievably selfish."[5] What is required in such cases is a willingness to find a "common ground" on which support can be given and received (perhaps through quiet, nonsexual holding), as well as an earnest attempt on the part of each spouse to reach out into the experience of the partner and reaffirm their connection in ways that "fit" for both.

We need to learn to honor and understand styles of mourning that are not our own.

Adapting to Loss: Ten Practical Steps

Although there are few hard and fast prescriptions about how to cope with loss, here are ten practical suggestions for dealing with the many losses with which life confronts us. Some of these strategies can be practiced well in advance of major losses, while others can only be used when adversity occurs—and in anticipation of the next. However, remember that loss and grief are highly personal experiences that do not suggest a single path for all mourners.

1. **Take the little losses seriously.** By taking time to show your caring for a friend who is moving away, or to experience the moment of sadness that comes in leaving a home grown too small or large for our present needs,

we give ourselves an opportunity to "rehearse" for the larger losses of our lives. Similarly, the death of a pet goldfish can be used as a "teachable moment" to instruct children on the meaning of death and its place in life, preparing them for future losses.

2. **Take time to feel.** Although major losses confront us with practical demands that make private reflection difficult to "sandwich in," build in quiet time to be alone and undistracted. Privately writing about our experiences and observations at moments of transition can contribute to a sense of release and understanding.

3. **Find healthy ways to relieve stress.** Almost be definition, transitions of any kind are stressful. Seek constructive ways to deal with this stress, whether through activity, exercise, relaxation training, or prayer.

4. **Make sense of your loss.** Rather than trying to push thoughts of your loss from your mind, allow yourself to obsess. Trying to banish painful images only gives them greater power. As you construct a coherent story of your experience, it will fall into greater perspective.

5. **Confide in someone.** Burdens shared are not as heavy. Find people—family members, friends, a pastor or therapist—who can hear what you are going through without introducing their own "agendas." Accept the caring gestures and listening ears of many others graciously, recognizing that your turn to reciprocate will come.

6. **Let go of the need to control others.** Other people affected by the loss will grieve it in their own way, and in their own time. Don't force them to conform to your particular pathway through mourning.

7. **Ritualize the loss in a personally significant way.** If the original funeral service for your loved one was unsatisfying, participate in planning a memorial service more in keeping with your needs. Find creative ways to memorialize nontraditional losses that fit the person you are and the transition you have undergone.

8. **Allow yourself to change.** Losses of people and roles central to our lives change us. Embrace these changes, finding those opportunities that exist for growth, however bittersweet it may be. Strive to enlarge yourself in the experience of loss, while also recognizing the senses in which it has reduced you.

9. **Harvest the legacy of the loss.** Reevaluate your life priorities, and search for opportunities to apply what the loss has taught you in future projects and relationships. Let your constructive reflections find expression in suitable actions, perhaps by reaching out to others in need.

10. **Center in your spiritual convictions.** Use the loss as an opportunity to review and renew your taken-for-granted religious and philosophical beliefs, and seek a deeper and well-tempered spirituality.

Reaching Out to Others

Statistics tell us that each death touches the lives of 128 survivors. With this in mind, it is more accurate to see ourselves as participants in a *grief system,* rather than as isolated individuals or even as compartmentalized families affected by loss. In all probability, someone we know well is currently grieving a major loss, whether through death, relationship dissolution, or life transition. Even though we ourselves may be affected by the same loss or a different one, we have the opportunity to reach out in support and understanding to that other in his or her personal time of need.

And yet, we are often reluctant to do so out of a fear of "not knowing what to say." Even when we do approach others in their grief, we tend to do so with the mistaken belief that it is our responsibility to "cheer them up" or give them "advice" on what they need to be doing to cope more effectively. Of course, there are times that they may approach us with just such a request, for a simple relaxing evening of light conversation, or for help with a complex financial problem. But more commonly, grieving individuals need something less tangible but more important—the opportunity to share their feelings and stories without feeling the press to either quickly move beyond their pain or find a "fast fix" for a problem that resists easy solutions.

I was angry. After all these years of marriage, he divorced me for a younger woman just w
expected we would be traveling and enjoying life together. I really appreciated my friend w
me be angry and didn't try to "fix it." She was there to hear me out and just be with m
—*Katherine, age 59*

When Bill left me, I felt so different than other mothers, like there was something wrong wi
But then I joined Parents Without Partners, and found out just how common my experien
feelings really were. It helped so much to know I was not alone.
—*Ruth, age 29*

Understandably, we sometimes seek to simplify the complex process of giving comfort to another by resorting to formulaic responses such as "I know just how you feel," "Time heals all wounds," or "God works in mysterious ways." Such responses often do more harm than good. In truth, we cannot presume to know how another feels about something so personal as a major loss—particularly if we have never given that person an opportunity to express his or her feelings to us in the first place. Nor is it true that time alone heals; instead, as we have seen above, mourning is an active process with many challenges, and the scar of the loss will in some sense be with the survivor forever. Even the attempt to provide support by describing the loss as "God's will" risks provoking anger and deepening the bereaved individual's spiritual crisis. If such phrases were indeed effective in assuaging the mourner's pain, then grieving would be an easier process than experience has taught us.

't say to me, "This happened because you're such a good strong family and God knows you can take it."

—Jackie, age 28

How then can we respond to another who is trying to meet the hard challenges posed by loss? There is only one "right" answer, and that is to do so personally and genuinely, being guided by your caring for that person and your willingness to hear and share the pain. Gentle openers that let the bereaved individual define the agenda can be helpful, such as "How are you feeling today?" or "Would you like to talk about it?" While your primary role will be to listen without intruding with quick answers or solutions, it is often appropriate to share something of your own experience of the lost loved one, perhaps a special memory or brief story that conveys something of his or her meaning to you. Remember that it is rarely the answers or recommendations that you offer that make a difference, but rather your ongoing availability to share the survivor's deepest thoughts and feelings.

One of the best supports we had was when somebody called us or wrote us or stopped in, and would talk about our son who was killed and would say something about him that they fou special. That was extraordinarily helpful.
                    —*Bob, age 44*

When I lost my job, I couldn't talk to my wife about it, because she was as anxious as I was kept pressing me to find another job right away. But my brother was real helpful at that tir because he just listened in an encouraging way, telling me he'd help out in any way he could. he meant it.
                    —*Ray, age 34*

When tangible assistance is clearly needed, do not be reluctant to offer it. A young widower will often need assistance with child care responsibilities, just as a young widow may need help with unfamiliar business arrangements surrounding the death of her husband. Divorced friends and family need to be included in social get-togethers rather than left out as the "fifth wheel." Of course, it is critical to avoid gender or age-related stereotypes in the forms of help we offer, allowing ourselves instead to be guided by our understanding of the persons to whom we are reaching out, or their answers to our question, "What would be the most help to you now?" When you offer help, be specific. The offer to "call me if you need anything" will seldom get a response, whereas the inquiry, "What night this week can I bring over dinner?" will more likely be met with an appreciative acceptance. Remember that the mourner's needs persist long after traditional support (in the form of the funeral or visitation) is withdrawn, and that periodic support, particularly over the first year following the loss, can help the person reconnect with a world that has been traumatically shattered.

Do's and Don'ts when Reaching Out to a Mourner

Don't:	*Do:*
Force the mourner into a role, by saying, "You're doing so well." Allow the mourner to have troubling feelings without the sense of letting you down.	**Open the door to communication.** If you aren't sure what to say, ask, "How are you feeling today?" or "I've been thinking about you. How is it going?"
Tell the mourner what he or she "should" do. At best, this reinforces the mourner's sense of incompetence, and at worst, your advice can be "off target" completely.	**Listen 80% of the time, and talk 20% of the time.** Very few people take the time to listen to someone's deepest concerns. Be one of the few. Both you and the mourner are likely to learn as a result.
Say, "Call me if you need anything." Vague offers are meant to be declined, and the mourner will pick up the cue that you implicitly hope he or she won't contact you.	**Offer specific help** and take the initiative to call a mourner. If you also respect the survivor's privacy, your concrete assistance with the demands of daily living will be appreciated.
Suggest that time heals all wounds. The wounds of loss never completely heal, and grief work is more active than this phrase suggests.	**Expect future "rough spots,"** with active attempts at coping with difficult feelings and decisions for months following the loss.
Delegate helping to others. Your personal presence and concern will make a difference.	**"Be there" for the mourner.** There are few rules for helping aside from openness and caring.
Say, "I know how you feel." Each griever's experience of grief is unique, so invite the mourner to share his or her feelings, rather than presuming that you know what the issues are for that person.	**Talk about your own losses** and how you adapted to them. Although the mourner's coping style may be different from your own, your self-disclosure will help.
Use hackneyed consolation, by saying,"There are other fish in the sea," or "God works in mysterious ways." This only convinces the mourner that you do not care enough to understand.	**Use appropriate physical contact**—like an arm around the shoulder or a hug—when words fail. Learn to be comfortable with shared silence, rather than chattering away in an attempt to cheer the person up.
Try to hurry the person through grief by urging that he or she get busy, give away the deceased's possessions, etc. Grief work takes time and patience and cannot be done on a fixed achedule.	**Be patient with the griever's story,** and allow him or her to share memories of the lost loved one. This fosters a healthy continuity as the person orients to a changed future.

Chapter 5 Research Notes

1. A broad "narrative revolution" has recently swept through psychology and related disciplines, whose central emphasis is understanding human beings in "storied" terms, in order to highlight the plot structure (significant events) and themes (latent meanings) of individual lives. Particularly relevant to the present argument is the development of narrative theories and techniques of psychotherapy, which are highly compatible with the constructivist framework for understanding loss delineated in Part 2. For a good scholarly introduction to narrative thinking, see Donald Polkinghorne's (1988), *Narrative knowing an the human sciences,* Albany: SUNY Press. Broad surveys of narrative psychotherapy can be found in Hugh Rosen and Kevin Kuehlwein's (1996) *Constructing realities,* San Francisco: Jossey Bass; and Robert Neimeyer and Michael Mahoney's (1995) *Constructivism in psychotherapy,* Washington, D.C.: American Psychological Association. Both of the latter books contain a diversity of constructivist and narrative approaches, and both provide clinical examples of a narrative model of practice.

2. Harvey has contributed one of the most important and spellbinding books integrating narrative material from the standpoint of grief recovery. In his 1996 book, *Embracing their memory,* Needham Heights, MA: Allyn & Bacon, he draws on research, scholarship, literature, and the personal experiences of many survivors of tragedy to underscore the therapeutic potential of "telling one's story" or constructing an account of the loss in the presence of understanding listeners.

3. See Terry Martin and Kenneth Doka (1996), Masculine grief. In K. Doka (Ed.), *Living with grief after sudden loss.* Washington: Hospice Foundation of America. These authors offer a number of useful suggestions for helping masculine grievers, including facilitation of their natural tendency toward problem-solving, reassurance that emotional loss of control is normal and temporary, encouragement for venting of anger, and respect for the survivor's need for privacy. A case study that follows these general guidelines appears in the second chapter of Part 2 of the present book.

4. See S. R. Shuchter and S. Zisook (1993), The course of normal grief. In M. Stroebe, W. Stroebe and R. O. Hansson (Eds.), *Handbook of bereavement: Theory, research, and intervention* (pp. 23-43). New York: Cambridge University Press.

5. These conclusions are drawn from the research of Reiko Schwab (1992), Effects of a child's death on the marital relationship, *Death Studies, 16,* 141-154. For further evocative descriptions of gender differences in grieving and their impact on marital intimacy, see Annelies Hagemeister & Paul C. Rosenblatt (1997), Grief and the sexual relationship of couples who have experienced a child's death, *Death Studies, 21,* 231-253. These issues are re-examined in the context of a discussion of the meaning reconstruction model in Part 2.

Chapter 6

Ritual and Renewal

So far, we have explored primarily the *personal* and *interpersonal* features of grief work, the emotional challenges that we confront alone or in the presence of a few family members or trusted friends. Yet grief work ultimately transcends these smaller contexts, and has communal dimensions as well. All known human societies have evolved patterned ceremonies for acknowledging the passing of their members, ceremonies that serve to reaffirm the formal and informal bonds among the survivors while also recognizing and honoring the contribution of the one who has died. This chapter will consider the ritualization of loss, and its psychological functions for those who go on living. While primary attention will be paid to the role of traditional funerals in giving meaning to loss, we will also consider briefly the role of personal rituals in the meaning-making process.

Functions of Ritual

Rituals punctuate life, publicly marking significant points of transition for the members of a community. Beginning with the shower for or baptism of a new baby, a seemingly endless series of rituals symbolize each step in our coming of age, from the annual birthday parties that celebrate each new year of life, through the graduation ceremonies that recognize our educational achievements, to wedding ceremonies that declare the love and commitment of two people, to the retirement parties that recognize a lifetime of devoted service in the world of work. As this list demonstrates, rituals can have a secular as well as spiritual dimension, drawing on varying balances of religious protocols (such as taking solemn marriage vows following a prescribed liturgy) and folk traditions (like drinking a champagne toast to the bride and groom) that are shared by the members of the community.

Like all social practices, however, the rituals that surround death evolve over time, and with the pace of change in contemporary society, the changes in our observances of loss have been rapid and significant. Especially in American culture, there has been a trend toward the *deritualization* of death and bereavement, as traditional practices such as elaborate funeral ceremonies, wakes, vigils, and modes of dress during bereavement have become hollow for many mourners and communities. Even for persons who find comfort and meaning in traditional observances, the character of many losses challenges their customary ritualization. For example, religious rites for those who have committed suicide or died of "stigmatizing" diseases such as AIDS may be problematic in some fundamental Christian congregations, and some mourners (e.g., a mistress of the deceased or an ex-husband) may be disenfranchised from participation in even "normal" funerals. [1] Moreover, while loss through death is openly commemorated in at least most cases with some form of ceremony, other losses (e.g., job loss) go wholly unnoticed in any public sense. In some cases this is subtly ironic: while elaborate rituals exist for commemorating the beginning of a marriage, none exist to acknowledge its ending. Thus, public rituals can sometimes fail us precisely because they are designed to affirm communal values (such as the legitimizing of heterosexual relationships in marriage, or career longevity), sometimes at the expense of individual needs.

In order to design rituals that are more adequate to all of our losses, it is important to understand their function more completely. Bronna Romanoff and Marion Terenzio have recently provided an eloquent discussion of rituals relevant to the grieving process, defining them as cultural devices that preserve the social order and provide ways of comprehending some of the most complex aspects of human existence. [2] Rituals, according to these authors, provide a pattern for our life cycle, a structure for our emotional chaos, a symbolic order for events, and a social construction of shared meanings. Like other rites of passage, funerals serve these functions while delimiting our grief and reaffirming our communal bonds. But along with more personal forms of ritualizing loss, they must attend to three dimensions in order to meet the needs of the bereaved. These include:

1. *Transformation of the mourner's sense of self,* while recasting one's attachment to the deceased. As an intrapsychic or personal process, this might entail giving the griever an opportunity to reflect on the role of the lost loved one in his or her life in a private moment at the grave site, or selecting and conferring a treasured memento to another affected by the death. The transformative aspects of ritual therefore acknowledge that one is changed by the loss, but also that the relationship with the deceased can be preserved in a symbolic form.

2. *Transition to a new social status.* This more "outward" process entails public recognition of the changed status of both the deceased (e.g., from a living participant in the community to someone present in spirit) and survivor (e.g., from wife to widow). While important for the community as a whole, this social transition does not necessarily imply the intrapsychic adjustments involved in the transformation process above.

3. *Connection to that which is lost,* as an alternative to "severing ties." For example, the Catholic anniversary Mass or Jewish Yizkor can foster such continued connection with the deceased in the corresponding cultural context, just as spontaneous or creative rituals (such as the custom of sharing stories or recollections of the deceased) can serve to consolidate survivors' memories of the one they lost, and recognize his or her continued influence on their lives. Several examples of rituals that serve this function are described below.

Alan Wofelt, a prominent grief counselor, has argued that the funeral ceremony helps us acknowledge the reality of the death, gives testimony to the life of the deceased, encourages the expression of grief in a way consistent with the culture's values, provides support to mourners, allows for the embracing of faith and beliefs about life and death, and offers continuity and hope for the living. In keeping with this perspective and the model of ritual transformation, transition, and continuation outlined by Romanoff and Terenzio, it can be useful to consider the ways in which the ritualization of loss can assist the bereaved in meeting the "challenges of mourning" outlined earlier in this book. We will first consider the ways in which funeral services can be enlisted to meet these challenges, and then turn to examples of personal rituals, perhaps enacted years after the loss, that can facilitate the ongoing task of adaptation.

———

The symbol of ritual provides us a means to express our beliefs and feelings when words alone not do those beliefs and feelings justice.
                                                    —*Alan D. Wofelt*

———

Acknowledge the reality of the death. By officially recognizing the passing of a member of the community, funeral services promote a public acknowledgment of the reality of the death, providing a permissive space and time in which the inward grief of survivors can be given outward form. Whether in the formal eulogy or in the informal conversations that precede and follow it, they also encourage the consolidation and sharing of memories and stories about the deceased, at the same time that they strengthen bonds of caring among the survivors. As in family discussions of the death, care should be taken to include children in the ceremony, preparing them in advance for what they will encounter. Excluding them from this form of public acknowledgment can further isolate them in their grieving process, and add a troubling sense of unreality to the loss of their loved one.

Sensitively conducted funerals can also promote the acknowledgment of the death on personal as well as public levels. During the funeral and subsequent burial or cremation, mourners begin the long process of saying good-bye to their loved one, and in the case of open casket services, have the last opportunity to view the physical presence of the person they have lost. As in all aspects of grief work, however, the funeral should be seen as presenting an opportunity to initiate this leave-taking, rather than a *requirement* to do so. Thus, while offering sufficient structure to guide the bereaved through the symbolic parting from the person who has died, the funeral ritual should be flexible enough to accommodate the many ways that individual mourners cope with the reality of the loss.

Open yourself to the pain. Mainstream American culture does not easily tolerate strong feelings, particularly those that accompany the despair of profound loss. [3] At its best, a well-conducted funeral gives greater allowance for the experience and expression of painful emotions, validating their appropriateness in the supportive presence of caring others. Moreover, funerals implicitly recognize that the concentration of such emotion cannot be sustained indefinitely, and provide a safe and time-limited environment in which they can be legitimately embraced. While practices obviously vary from one subculture or family to another, the multifaceted character of most death observances (e.g., including visitation by family, friends, and clergy, burial or interment, and memorial services) typically prompt both recognition of shared sadness regarding the death, and opportunities for solace and consolation. Ideally, then, the difficult roller coaster of grieving can be modulated by both death rituals and the persons who participate in them.

Revise your assumptive world. It is all too easy in the course of daily life to live within the cozy conventions of a taken-for-granted system of beliefs. We assume that we will live a full life, that we can plan for a distant future with our loved ones, that good efforts will be rewarded, that life will treat us fairly. We can even believe in a straightforward theology that assumes that God will answer requests in the way we would like, or that guardian angels will protect ourselves and our loved ones from harm if we live righteous lives. In all of these ways, we tend to live day to day as if the universe had a simple order that can be discerned by human minds, and that permits us a substantial degree of predictability and control as long as we "play by the rules."

The intrusion of traumatic loss into our lives cruelly shatters all of these illusions. We learn that lives can be cut short, that the future (even tomorrow) is not assured, and that bad things can happen to good people. Moreover, major loss can lead us to question a childlike theology that casts God as a protective or indulgent paternal figure, producing a crisis of meaning for which no simple answers will suffice. Above all, traumatic loss introduces a terrible sense of randomness into our lives, stripping us of the sense of control over our ultimate destinies that we might once have comfortably assumed.

The funeral, as a rite of passage, not only makes vivid the hard lessons of loss, but also can initiate a process of rebuilding an assumptive world that has been shattered by death. A moving liturgy can help reconnect mourners to their bedrock faith, or prompt them toward a deeper level of spiritual awakening as they begin the search for a more mature personal philosophy. It also confronts us with the inescapable reality of death and human limitation, which can serve as a catalyst to seeking meaning in our lives day-to-day, rather than deferring important matters to a future day that is not guaranteed. If we can come to accept at an emotional as well as intellectual level that we, too, will die, then we can be liberated to "make today count," rather than running from the awareness of our finitude through a pursuit of material success and achievement. To the extent that we frantically run away from death in an effort to avoid it, we distract ourselves from the deeper lessons of our mortality. By putting us back in touch with our own finitude, the funeral and burial service can reacquaint us with the deeper possible meanings of our lives, and prompt us to reach for more sustaining values.

Reconstruct your relationship to that which has been lost. As our relationship to the deceased is transformed by death to one based on symbolic rather than physical interaction, we become increasingly reliant on our fund of memories of our loved one to keep the relationship "alive." The eulogy that occurs during the funeral service assists with this task, recapitulating the major achievements of the person's life to give it a sense of wholeness and coherence for all those attending. More importantly, the informal recollections and stories shared before, during, and after the formal ceremony may consolidate precious memories for the primary mourners, or reveal new dimensions of the loved one that were unique to certain relationships. For many families, the physical reminders of the ceremony—the program for the service or the flag draped over the casket of a veteran prior to burial—become precious mementos that serve as cherished "linking objects" that connect the living to the dead, granting a sense of continuity to the survivors. While personally significant ways of memorializing the loss may be practiced long after the burial, the funeral often provides concrete assistance in meeting this particular challenge of mourning.

Reinvent yourself. Of all the tasks of mourning, perhaps the most fundamental is that of reconstructing a new identity appropriate to the bereaved individual's changed status. In a very real sense, we are no longer who we once were prior to the loss, in so far as our sense of self is closely identified with our most intimate relationships. As a formal rite of passage, the funeral ushers in and validates this change in status of the central mourners in the eyes of the community, a change that is symbolized in various ways ranging from a prescribed manner of dress to customs of greeting and comforting.

As in the challenge of reconstructing one's relationship to the deceased, the task of "relearning the self," as Attig calls it, continues in the months and years following the rites of the funeral. But it is at the funeral that this task most visibly begins, and where tangible and symbolic social support for the new identity is provided by the community of grievers.

Personal Rituals

While funeral services represent the clearest form of loss ritual sanctioned by our society, and can assist with healthy grieving in all of the ways outlined above, they are rarely adequate to fully memorialize a death in the minds of survivors. Even more critically, no communal rites of any kind exist for other types of losses (horrendous deaths, miscarriages, divorces, property loss, assault, illness), leaving those who suffer them without the support of ritual assistance in giving form and legitimacy to their grief and facilitating its resolution.

For these reasons, other forms of ritual can be helpful in further honoring the continued importance of loved ones who have died, or in validating the significance of losses other than through death. At a communal level, commemorative ceremonies for those who died in military action (D-Day ceremonies, or community observances on the anniversaries of a mass tragedy or bombing) serve this function, as do group pilgrimages to such shrines as the Vietnam War Memorial or the Holocaust Museum. Of course, individual participation in such activities can also contribute to personal and spiritual growth, even for those participants who were only vaguely aware of the sacrifices made by previous generations, whether or not those who died were members of one's own family or cultural group.

When I visited the American Holocaust Museum, I walked through the chronology of the Jew
people in Europe, from the development of their community in pre-Hitler Germany, through
first outbreaks of violence during Kristalnacht, to the incredible horrors of the "Final Solution
I wended my way from the early exhibits on the upper floors of the museum to the lower floor
images, and even the lighting, I think, became darker. By the time I reached the death camps,
as numbed and horrified as those poor people must have. When I finally finished the exhibit
walked from the museum into the light of day, I felt like I too had died and been reborn. As lo
I live I'll never forget that experience.
                                                                    —Karen, age 45

On a smaller scale, but no less significant level, families and individuals
can create meaningful ways of memorializing or honoring their own losses,
whether by including those who have died in a Thanksgiving prayer, giving a
charitable contribution in honor of a lost loved one, or years after a death,
holding a memorial service that provides an opportunity for real participation of the survivors in a way that the original ceremony did not. Losses can
be recognized in less conventional ways as well, by creating a family crest,
having a "dialogue" with a deceased loved one in a personal journal, or undertaking genealogical research to construct a family tree. One young couple,
following the accidental death of their youngest child, decided to celebrate
his life each subsequent year by declaring his birthday "Family Day." Each
year on this special day, both parents took off work, and both of the other
children skipped school, in order to spend the whole day doing something
enjoyable together, whether hiking, going to the zoo, or simply working together to prepare a special meal and share reminiscences about their son or
brother. Because such observances are not tied to the time of death, they can
be drawn upon years later to help heal open wounds, say good-bye, renew a
symbolic relationship with the deceased, or promote family communication
about earlier losses in ways that were not possible at the time the death occurred. [4]

———

he Christmas after my father died, my mother and all of us adult children again came together
t my parent's cabin in the woods, just as we always had for as long as I could remember. We
ughed and cried a lot that year, and none of us really knew what to do about Dad not being
e. Finally, after the dinner, we were sitting around and talking, and everybody just kind of fell
t. Then it hit me what was missing. Every year after dinner, my Dad, who had learned to love
animals he once hunted, would put on his huge orange hunting jacket and go hiking through
woods to keep the hunters off of his property; when we were little we used to go with him. And
got up, went to the closet, and found that big orange jacket, put it on, and headed out. I think
vas good for all of us. Everybody started kidding me about going on "Bambi patrol," just like
ey did him, and I spent some sad, quiet hours that day walking through the woods with my
ther. I felt so close to him, almost like he was holding me in his big arms as we walked along.
—Jackie, age 35

———

One of the more moving of these alternative memorials, which literally weaves together the individual and communal levels of recognition, is the Names Project AIDS quilt. In it, families and loved ones who have lost someone to the disease sew, embroider, paint, or soft-sculpt a square honoring the one who has died, often with highly personal messages like, "Dear Brian— Save the last dance for me." These individual squares are then stitched into the fabric of one of the enormous panels that make up the quilt. Some sense of the immensity of our loss to this disease as a nation can be gleaned from the sheer size of the quilt, which more than covered the entire area of the Mall in Washington, D.C., during an earlier display in that city. The high degree of personalism and collaboration embodied in the quilt in a sense represent the ideal form of ritual recognition, integrating individual expression of the meaning of a loss into a communal product that gives it lasting significance.

Finally, nontraditional losses are no less deserving of ritual recognition. Pets can be honored with a burial service rather than mere disposal, perhaps giving children a special opportunity to participate through artistic "gifts," poems, or eulogies commemorating what the beloved animal had meant to them [5]. Symbolic rites of passage can also be constructed to acknowledge the sad transitions that sometimes temper us, and make us who we are. A man who finds himself drinking too much following a painful divorce that separates him from his children may symbolically "throw away the bottle," resolving to become the kind of man his children would respect were they to reunite. Two brothers in young adulthood can visit their family home in another state, from which they moved at a point of family crisis decades before. A woman may organize a family reunion, in a symbolic effort to bridge old rifts among family members about issues that are now nearly forgotten. In these and a thousand other ways, individuals and families can construct rituals that connect them with that which they have lost and to those who shared the loss with them. In so doing, they open themselves to the paradoxical power of loss, to both diminish and enrich our lives.

Grief is the process of moving from losing what we have, to having what we've lost.
—Stephen Fleming

---

pter 6 Research Notes

1. The exclusion of emotionally involved but socially disenfranchised mourners from funeral observances is vividly depicted in the opening sequence of the musical film *Evita,* in which Eva Perón as the "illegitimate" child of a prominent man is physically barred from attending his funeral. While the sanctions against such participation may have relaxed somewhat in our own culture, it is nonetheless true that traditional funerals exclude many to whom the bereaved has been important (e.g., ex-lovers), effectively confirming the significant status of some mourners while denying that of others.

2. See Bronna Romanoff and Marion Terenzio (1998), Rituals and the grieving process, *Death Studies,* in press. While their primary goal is to expand on the concept of rituals as "rites of passage" to include processes of transformation and continuation as well as transition, their model is highly relevant to the practical ritualization of loss, as developed in this chapter and later sections of this book.

3. I qualify this statement by emphasizing the practices of mainstream white culture, insofar as very different patterns of grieving are permitted and even encouraged among African American and Latino cultures. For a moving portrayal of the emotionally expressive and communal practices typical of traditional black families in the South, see Annette Dula (1997), The story of Miss Mildred. In K. Doka (Ed.), *Living with grief: When illness is prolonged.* Washington, DC: Hospice Foundation of America.

4. Several additional ritual forms that can be modified for individual circumstances are presented in the *Personal Applications* section contained in the present book, as well as in the practical article by Craig Vickio entitled, Together in spirit: Keeping our relationships alive when loved ones die. *Death Studies,* in press, 1998. An example of the therapeutic facilitation of leave-taking rituals (in the form of helping a client progressively say "good-bye" to her father through visiting places intimately associated with his life) can be found in Robert Neimeyer (1996), Process interventions for the constructivist

psychotherapist. In H. Rosen and K. Kuehlwein (Eds.), *Constructing realities.* San Francisco: Jossey Bass.

5. Following the death of his beloved Siberian dwarf hamster, my four-year old son Michael wrote the following poem to commemorate the life of his little friend, which he buried in the backyard in Fluffy's shoebox casket. In kindergarten spelling, he wrote:

> Fluffy was our favrit pet
> And our loving too.
> We wish he was nu.

He also wanted his picture taken holding Fluffy one last time before his burial. On the other hand, my seven year old son, Eric, preferred not to participate in this little ritual, but wanted a detailed explanation of why Fluffy had died and my opinion about whether he had suffered. Such examples reinforce the points that children can be full (and sometimes central) participants in the ritualization of death, and that allowance must be made for individual modes of accommodating the large and small losses that life inevitably entails.

Part 2:

For Those Who Help

Chapter 7

Meaning Reconstruction and the
Experience of Loss

———

Until she was 34, Kerry led what she had always considered a "charmed" life. Relatively affluent and outgoing, she had been popular among her peers through high school, and in her early 20's, married for the first time to begin the family she had always wanted. Even her divorce from what she later conceded to be this "premature" marriage did little to perturb a life filled with the external rewards of abundance and social belongingness. While she sometimes harbored inner doubts that she lacked the "depth" and "love" she sometimes perceived in others, for the most part her life remained "easy and beautiful" as it progressed along a predictable course of social and community involvement. Her second marriage, to her college sweetheart, seemed to confirm the "normality" of her life, as she gave birth to a healthy daughter, and a few years later, conceived a son.

Then, with the birth of her son, Jacob, all this changed. For the next two years Kerry found herself to be the primary caretaker to an infant with a congenital heart defect, alternately embracing and resenting the constant vigilance and sacrifice that this entailed. Every few weeks for the two years her son lived, Kerry would detect further symptoms of heart failure in Jacob, and accompany him to the hospital praying that some miracle would be performed, or some medication would be administered that would allow her to return to the normal life she craved for her and her family. But night after night, as she lay crying and "thrashing" on a hospital cot in her son's room, she found these prayers unanswered. Even with the occasional support of friends and family, she felt trapped in an exhausting and emotionally draining existence, displaced from the people, patterns, and projects that had once given her life a familiar, if sometimes superficial, form. When Jacob died during the last of these lengthy hospitalizations, Kerry felt disoriented and inconsolable, and struggled for an answer for what it had all meant, both for herself and her family. She found no easy answers.

At age 76, Clara had built a life on self-sacrifice. The third of four children in a conservative Jewish family, Clara learned and internalized the historical suffering of her people, and came to view devotion to one's purpose and loyalty to others as the ultimate guiding principles of life. As a young woman, she had entered the nursing profession, working in a medical environment that frequently demanded that she place her own needs behind those of others who needed her to "be there" for them when they were helpless to help themselves. Clara's personal life reinforced these existential commitments, as she devoted herself to raising three children of her own without the support of her "workaholic" husband, while simultaneously providing in-home care for his mother during the slow years of deterioration leading to her death.

Now, in late life, Clara faced a dilemma for which she could find no solution. Her husband, Ed, lay "dying by degrees" in a nursing home, having suffered a series of strokes that left him disabled, noncommunicative, and semilucid much of the time. Perhaps the only constant in his personality was his anger and combativeness: long abusive to her both emotionally and physically, he now fluctuated between crying like a small child and raging wildly at perceived injustices in his treatment by both the nursing home staff and Clara herself. Clara left these daily visits feeling "tortured and depressed," to the point of contemplating suicide as the only way out of the insoluble "trap" represented by her need to care for a man who both begged for and rejected her attempts at caretaking. To complicate her situation, Clara's oldest son, Richard, had become increasingly forceful in demanding that she discontinue her evidently painful visitation to a father he had resented all his life. Unable to behave in so "selfish" a manner, Clara now began to feel estranged from the "son who loved her most," as well from the helpless husband who apparently hated her.

As we strive to understand the many forms of loss and their impact on survivors, we are quickly pushed to the limits of our conventional models of grief and bereavement. As human beings struggling with seemingly inhuman demands, we all too often find ourselves caricatured in the overly simple portrayal of grief offered by traditional "stage" theories of adaptation to loss. Not only do these theories seem strangely anonymous in their description of supposedly universal symptoms of grief and phases of emotional reactions, but they also seem to miss the particulars of our struggle, and its embeddedness in a life that is uniquely our own. As I have tried across time to come to terms with the losses in my own life and in the lives of those persons I have counseled, I have been led to question the adequacy of conventional grief theory as a description of our efforts to accommodate to the deaths of those we love, and as a framework for assisting others to adapt to a world that is forever transformed by their passing. These efforts have gradually led me to an alternative view, one that is shared by a small but growing group of clinicians, theorists, and researchers concerned with bereavement. This view, which resonates with what has been termed a constructivist approach to psychotherapy [1], takes as its fundamental assumption that *the attempt to reconstruct a world of meaning is the central process in the experience of grieving.* In this brief chapter, I will sketch a few propositions that derive from this view, drawing on the particulars of Kerry and Clara's cases to illustrate its implications for our work with those who are engaged in this process. Thus, this chapter builds on some of the themes woven through Part 1 of this book, particularly those emphasizing rebuilding our assumptive world, redefining ourselves both psychologically and socially, and finding meaningful ways to symbolize for ourselves and others the transitions we have undergone in the course of our bereavement.

tional Models of Grief and Their Limitations

A common denominator of most traditional theories of grief is their identification of a series of stages or phases of adjustment, beginning with the actual or imminent death of a loved one, and progressing through various forms of emotional reaction until the bereaved individual achieves some form of recovery, reconciliation, or the like. While stage models of the phenomenology of mourning can be traced at least to the work of Lindemann [2], who subdivided grief into the stages of shock-disbelief, acute mourning, and resolution, the most influential of these theories is that proposed by Kübler-Ross, whose 1969 book, *On Death and Dying* has been translated into more languages than the Bible. The focus of Kübler-Ross's work was the emotional transition (beginning with denial, and progressing through anger, bargaining, and depression, before eventuating in possible acceptance) experienced by terminal patients anticipating their own deaths, although it has since been generalized (probably inappropriately) to a model of the grief process among survivors as well [3]. Most subsequent stage models of bereavement have drawn upon some combination or variation of these two sequences, as has my own preliminary attempt in Chapter 1 to describe the phases in adjustment to loss in terms of *avoidance, assimilation,* and *accommodation*. Simple step-by-step models of this kind are appealing for their clarity, a factor that has contributed to their widespread appeal among both professionals and lay persons striving to understand the complexities of loss.

While some indirect support for a stage theory of mourning can be derived from comparative developmental research on loss, most research on grieving has failed to find evidence for the validity and reliability of such a model. [4] Specifically, research has provided little empirical support for the presence of distinct psychological stages, much less for a determined sequence of psychological states. Following loss, many people do not demonstrate the proposed states at all or do not experience them in an identifiable sequence. Instead, the particular form of response and the sequence and duration of emotional reactions to loss vary greatly between individuals. [5]

The paucity of empirical evidence to support stage models as well as my clinical observations and personal experience with loss have led me to reject many of the implicit assumptions of traditional grief theories, and to turn away from some of the clinical practices derived from such assumptions. I no longer assume that people experience a universal sequence of stages or tasks following loss or that the process of grieving can usefully be viewed as eventuating in an end state of "recovery." I do not believe that the bereaved passively negotiate a train of psychological transitions forced upon them by external events. I cannot endorse the implication that a normative pattern of grieving can be prescriptive or diagnostic, and that deviations from such a course are to be considered "abnormal" or "pathological." More subtly, I would question whether emotional responses should be considered the primary focus of our grief theories, to the exclusion or minimization of behavior and meaning. And finally, I have doubts about the individualistic bias of traditional theories of bereavement, which tend to construe grief as an entirely private act, experienced outside the context of human relatedness. All of these concerns have prompted me toward an alternative model of grieving, predicated on a constructivist or narrative theory of meaning reconstruction in the wake of significant loss. After outlining some of the design criteria for such a theory, I will offer a few "working notes" toward its assumptive structure, considering its relevance for grief therapy and grief counseling along the way.

gn Criteria for a Useful Grief Theory

From a constructivist perspective, a useful theory of grief would need to meet a number of criteria which stand in contrast to traditional theories. First, it would reveal the personal reality of death or loss for different individuals, instead of assuming that death holds a universal significance for human beings irrespective of their historical, cultural, familial, or personal contexts. Rather than forcing individuals into a nomothetic mold, it would be flexible enough to illuminate highly idiosyncratic constructions of death and their changes over time. Second, it would view people as active in facing death's challenges rather than being passive reactors. In practical terms, this implies that our models of loss should sensitize us to the variegated ways in which individuals and human collectives anticipate loss and assimilate it into personal and shared systems of belief. Third, the theory should be richly descriptive in elucidating personal meanings of loss, without being subtly prescriptive of what constitutes "normal" grieving. Clinically, it should position the counselor or therapist to explore the limitations and entailments of any particular construction of loss, without idealizing or pathologizing its distinctive form or structure. Fourth, it would focus on passionately held meanings that shape our emotional, behavioral, and somatic responses. Thus, rather than viewing grief preemptively in terms of the emotional sequelae of loss, it would provide a more holistic depiction of adaptation to bereavement. Fifth, it would describe how one's world is forever transformed by loss rather than suggesting a return to some premorbid state following a "recovery." By extension, our models should permit us to trace changes in the bereaved individual's self and life that do not simply reduce to a reestablishment of pre-loss patterns. Finally, while maintaining a focus on the highly personal qualities of grief, a useful theory would allow for the consideration and emplotment of grief in larger social and family contexts. Having outlined some fundamental criteria for a useful theory of grief, let us now turn to several propositions that my colleagues and I have found useful in scaffolding our research and clinical practice, and which we hope will foreshadow a more comprehensive theory of grieving conceived along constructivist lines.

A Propositional Beginning

As a relatively recent epistemology of clinical practice, constructivism views human beings as inveterate meaning-makers, striving to punctuate, organize, and anticipate their engagement with the world by construing it in terms of themes that express their particular cultures, families, and personalities. At an individual level, this suggests that persons construct idiosyncratic systems of meaning, organized around a set of core assumptions, which both govern their perception of life events and channel their behavior in relation to them. However, in contrast to more rationalistic cognitive theories that regard such interpretations of experience as "irrational" or "dysfunctional" to the extent that they fail to mirror "objective" reality, constructivism suggests that human beings have no simple recourse to a reality beyond their grasp, and instead must judge the viability of their constructions on the basis of their practical utility, their internal coherence, and their degree of consensual validation by relevant others. One implication of this position is that the concept of psychological "disorder" becomes relativized, insofar as different individuals and communities may adopt quite different criteria for judging any particular construction of events to be valid or invalid, functional or dysfunctional. In general, however, people seek to construct meaning systems that are internally consistent, socially supported, and that offer a degree of security in helping them anticipate and participate in the important experiences that comprise the narratives of their lives. Thus, any given construction can be considered problematic to the extent that it fails to do so. [6]

Adopting this basic constructivist position as a starting point for a theory of loss suggests several propositions, which collectively begin to sketch an alternative framework for understanding the adaptive processes entailed in grieving. Of course, I recognize that other grief theorists have also found traditional theories wanting, and have begun to work toward more adequate models of mourning that share features with the approach I outline in this paper. Indeed, I suspect that the field as a whole is gradually moving toward a new paradigm for understanding profound loss and its role in human life, and I hope that the present work will make a modest contribution to this reorientation. For this reason, within the limits of the space available, I will draw attention to the work of other authors that dovetails with my own, and that helps provide a conceptual platform for designing new principles and procedures for the practice of grief therapy.

As a starting point for this work, I will outline six straightforward propositions that are compatible with a constructivist position, and that together offer a fresh vantage point from which to view human mortality and bereavement. While I will occasionally cite research that supports these propositions or that demonstrates their importance in the grieving process, I offer these less as a distillation of research results than as an assumptive frame to guide the development of novel predictions and practices relevant to bereavement. [7]

1. Death as an event can validate or invalidate the constructions on the basis of which we live, or it may stand as a novel experience for which we have no constructions.

If we view human beings as constructing a unique world of meaning, then we need to understand the ways in which death can enter that world, confirming or disconfirming those constructions that give human lives their direction. In the course of daily living, each of us ordinarily is sustained by the network of habitual explanations, expectations, and enactments that shape our lives with others. These tacit assumptions provide us with a basic sense of order regarding our pasts, familiarity regarding our current relationships, and predictability regarding our futures. Experiences of loss that fit the contours of our constructions (as in the "appropriate" death of an elderly relative after a life well lived, or the "heroic" death of a warrior who martyrs himself for a cause we passionately support) can provide powerful validation for our assumptive worlds, whereas forms of death that are discrepant with our core constructions (e.g., the suicide of a loved one or the chronic suffering and death of a spouse or child) can challenge the adequacy of our most cherished beliefs and taken-for-granted ways of living. In the latter case the degree of reconstruction of our patterns of interpreting, anticipating, and organizing our lives may be profound, and may never be fully accomplished from the death of our loved one until our own. From a constructivist standpoint, what is crucial is the extent to which a particular form of death or loss articulates with our current ways of integrating experience, rather than the "objective" characteristics of the death itself. By implication, it is misleading to describe particular forms of death (e.g., violent, sudden) as inherently traumatic for survivors, except insofar as they are radically at odds with the constructions of that individual, family, or community.

In emphasizing the degree to which death supports or challenges our preexisting constructions of life, we are building upon the work of theorists such as Colin Murray Parkes [8], who defined our assumptive worlds as the "internal models" against which we match incoming data in order to orient the self, recognize what is happening, and plan behavior. While this "information processing" interpretation may suggest that human beings operate in a highly cognitive and self-aware fashion, Therese Rando clarifies that most of our assumptions "translate into virtually automatic habits of cognition and behavior," such that we might be quite unaware of the implicit expectations that we attach to a given relationship until we lose it. [9]

While some valuable research conducted from this perspective associates traumatic loss with disruptions of general schemas for interpreting life events (e.g., viewing the world as benevolent, life as meaningful, and the self as worthy), it may actually be equally revealing to reverse this emphasis, and to consider the extent to which distinctive ways of interpreting loss can mitigate or exacerbate its impact. For example, qualitative research by Mildred

Braun and Dale Berg has found that grief symptomatology was lower for mothers who could assimilate the deaths of their children into a preexisting philosophical or spiritual belief system, just as Elizabeth Milo found that mothers who lost developmentally disabled children following chronic illness coped better when they could find personal significance in their children's lives, suffering, and deaths. [10] Such research underscores the extent to which a particular loss can be given meaning within the framework of one's existing constructions, or appears to undermine this very framework.

While research on the assumptive world of grievers moves in the right direction, it often lacks attention to meaning-making activity at a highly personal level, a level not easily reduced to a general search for an image of the world as just, the self as worthy, and life events as meaningful. For example, Jacob's protracted illness and death invalidated Kerry's view of life as something that was relatively easy and abundant, confronting her with month after month of painful evidence that her previous way of living was inadequate to her current challenges. Not only did her preexisting philosophy of life leave her unprepared for the tragic complications resulting from her son's congenital illness, but his death also triggered a deep-going reevaluation of her priorities, her relationships, and even her sense of herself as a person. It is this inevitable individuality of meaning-making in the face of death and loss that is underscored in the second proposition.

2. Grief is a personal process, one that is idiosyncratic, intimate, and inextricable from our sense of who we are.

Grief can only be fully understood in the context of the everyday process of constructing, maintaining, and changing our most basic sense of self. Our personalities, outlooks, and dispositions are determined neither by our genes nor our environment, but by our own investment in those persons, places, projects and possessions to which we are bound by bonds of caring attachment. We organize our identities as we go along, consolidating a sense of self and world by building personal theories or interpretations of experiences with which life confronts us. When events shake our sense of self and world, we respond by trying to interpret them in ways consistent with our overall theories and identities. When these attempts fail, and our most basic sense of self is assaulted, we lose our secure grip on familiar reality, and are forced to reestablish another.

This proposition carries several implications for our conceptualization of grief and our assessment of its impact on individuals. To the extent that grief is shaped by these deeply personal processes of meaning making, it may be difficult to capture in common language, either for the speaker or listener. It may be especially hard to translate such disruption into standard "clinical" terminology or the rigid language of stages. This presents us as caregivers with a challenge to tune in to the more idiosyncratic and intimate meanings of loss, often forcing us to move beyond hackneyed expressions of support or preconceived ideas of what a particular loss "feels like" to any given griever. Instead, a deepened appreciation of the particularity of loss prompts us to listen intently for clues as to the unique significance of a bereavement experience for each client, which might be conveyed more adequately in metaphors or imagery than in the lexicon of public speech.

The intimacy required to explore and name the multiple losses associated with any given death must be earned rather than assumed, and premature attempts to offer a "clinical diagnosis" or even "helpful advice" will typically distance us as caregivers from the griever's experience. Most basically, we need to appreciate more deeply the extent to which losses of those we love (or even those we hate) can occasion profound shifts in our sense of who we are, as whole facets of our past that were shared with the deceased slip away from us forever, if only because no one else will ever occupy the unique position in relation to us necessary to call them forth. It is in this sense that grieving entails not only a process of relearning a world disrupted by loss, but relearning the self as well, in Attig's apt phrase.

Some of the intricacy of this process is suggested by Clara's attempt to come to terms with the chronic disability and impending death of her husband. Having constructed an identity based on a lifetime of selfless giving to others—perhaps to the point of martyrdom—she found herself unable either to resolve decades of "unfinished business" with Ed in the final months of his life, or to reconstrue her relationship with him. The same meaning system that had enabled her to survive the adversity of her earlier years now seemed to constrain her from living with some sense of acceptance and peace late in life. Empathically grasping and communicating this dilemma that derived from her construction of herself and her marriage provided an entry point into her world of meaning, and enabled me to begin to explore alternative symbolic ways of "finishing the conversation" with Ed, and allowing her to affirm her core identity by redirecting her caring toward others.

3. *Grieving is something we do, not something that is done to us.*

Clearly, bereavement as such is a "choiceless event," insofar as few of us would choose to lose those we love. As such, we experience it as an unwelcome intruder in our lives, one who refuses to retreat despite our impassioned protests. The power of death can leave us feeling helpless and overwhelmed, and we may experience ourselves as pawns in a cosmic game that eludes our best attempts at understanding.

And yet, while the loss of those we love through death may be a hard reality that we are powerless to avert, the experience of grieving itself may be rich in choice. At the most basic level we have a choice of whether to attend to the distress occasioned by our loss, to feel and explore the grief of our loved one's absence, or to disattend to or suppress our private pain and focus instead on adaptation to a changed external reality. This vacillation between engaging versus avoiding intensive "grief work" is fundamental to the "dual process" model of grieving proposed by Margaret Stroebe and her colleagues,[11] and relative emphases on one or the other of these processes may help account for the wide variation in mourning behavior found in different cultures.

At a more specific level, grieving involves hundreds of concrete choices, including whether to shoulder the burden of caring for an ailing loved one or delegate this responsibility to others, whether to view the body of the deceased, whether to keep or dispose of the loved one's possessions, whether to continue to live in a home once shared with the one who has died, how and with whom to share one's account of the loss, whether to ritualize the death and if so in what fashion, and how to continue to relate to one's internal representation or "spirit" of the lost loved one. Thus, far from representing a passive process of "waiting out" a series of predictable emotional transitions, grieving needs to be seen more realistically as a period of accelerated decision making (on both existential and practical levels), to the point that the bereaved individual may sometimes feel overwhelmed by the challenges posed.

Conceiving of grief as an intensely active process seems valuable to us not only because it seems to correspond more closely to the experience of actual grievers, but also because it gives more potential direction to grief therapists, who can play a facilitative role in sensitizing clients to the many subtle decisions they face and in helping them sift through the implications of their (conscious or unconscious) choices.

Clara's predicament illustrates the paradoxical nature of choice and the necessarily active process of accommodating to loss. As an objective reality, Ed's illness was clearly not consciously "chosen" by Clara, although at a less conscious level she may have found herself wishing for his death at any of a number of points during his abusive and domineering marriage to her. But now, faced with his post-stroke disability, she seemed surrounded by choices that overwhelmed her. Should she have him transferred to a Jewish nursing home, threatening her increasingly tenuous financial stability, or continue to have him cared for in a secular facility and risk the approbation of the members of her extended family and synagogue? Should she listen to the urgings of her son, and stop "torturing herself" by "sneaking out" to visit her dying but belligerent husband, or remain true to her marital vows to remain committed to Ed until "death do them part?" Perhaps most urgently, should she—and could she—manage to somehow go on living in the face of such dilemmas, or take the "coward's way out" by ending her own life, even at the cost of bringing shame to her family? In her case as in others, much of the work of therapy consisted in "deconstructing" these questions in such a way that they could lead to more optimistic answers, and permit her to focus on the less paralyzing process of reconstructing a life for herself following her husband's death.

4. Grieving is the act of affirming or reconstructing a personal world of meaning that has been challenged by loss.

To the extent that loss invalidates the assumptive structure of our lives in highly individualistic ways, challenging us to cope adaptively with a tumult of subjective experiences and objective demands, it requires us to reconstruct a world that again "makes sense," that restores a semblance of meaning, direction, and interpretability to a life that is forever transformed.

As a constructivist, I find a narrative model helpful in understanding this process of meaning reconstruction, which I regard as the central dynamic of grieving. If life is viewed as a story —albeit one we write with our actions and commitments as well as with words—then loss can be viewed as disrupting the continuity of this narrative, posing the threat of radical incoherence in the pre- and post-loss account. Like a novel that loses a central supporting character in a middle chapter, the life disrupted by bereavement forces its "author" to envision potentially far-reaching changes in plot in order for the story to move forward in an intelligible fashion. Moreover, chronic and protracted losses may gradually erode the plot structure of the "text" of one's biography, requiring continual revisions in the direction of one's life narrative, just at the point that we as authors have found a point of tenuous predictability. In such cases, constructing a way of continually bridging the past with a changing and uncertain future can be a major task, one that may require therapeutic support.

While complicated losses may "dislocate" us from the broader narrative of our lives in this sense, "adaptive" processes of reconstruction are also possible. [12] On the one hand, we can assimilate loss into pre-existing frameworks of meaning, ultimately reasserting the viability of the belief system that previously sustained us, or we can accommodate our life narrative to correspond more closely to what we perceive as a changed reality. The bereaved individual who integrates the protracted and painful death of a spouse into a long-held religious view emphasizing divine providence would illustrate the former assimilative process, whereas the mourner who is prompted by such a death to jettison, revise, or deepen his or her prior convictions would exemplify the latter accommodative process. Both movements may be adaptive in the sense that they reaffirm or reestablish a broad narrative structure within which tragedy can be given personal meaning.

Assimilative processes of meaning making are most evident in the case of Clara, who approached her husband's tempestuous dying trajectory by integrating it into the same system that had served her for as long as she could remember. Thus, she attempted to deal with it as yet another form of hardship to be endured loyally, selflessly "being there" for another at the expense of disattending to her own needs. However, this well-practiced construction of her role seemed inadequate in the face of the emotional demands of caring for and witnessing the progressive demise of a man she loved, but also powerfully resented. Kerry, in contrast, recognized more and more clearly with each month of her son's illness that the previous structure of her life was inadequate to the task of interpreting, much less giving meaningful direction, to the alien world in which she now found herself. Casting about for explanations for her family's suffering, she came to see it as a God-given chance to atone for her own "unconsciousness," to live less superficially and with greater self-awareness than she had in the past. In accepting this challenge, Kerry turned away from many of the trivial preoccupations that had once characterized her existence, and began to reorder her relationships and priorities in a way that accorded with her new sense of self. [13] Significantly for both women, their eventual reorganization was ushered in by a profound dislocation from their previous construction of life, precipitating them into painful self-examination until a new and fragile order began to emerge.

Construing bereavement in narrative terms is more than a metaphor; it carries concretely helpful implications for how grieving can be viewed and facilitated in a therapeutic context. At the most general level, a narrative view places emphasis on the centrality of "account-making," the way in which we spontaneously seek opportunities to tell and retell the stories of our loss, and in so doing, recruit social validation for the changed story lines of our lives. More specifically, it suggests several novel "narrative means to therapeutic ends," including the clinical use of specially adapted forms of journalling, poetic writing, and graphic recounting to help consolidate the many implications of loss and integrate them more completely into our ongoing life with others. [14] In this way constructivism provides not only specific techniques to facilitate processes of meaning-making in the face of invalidating life events, but also a framework within which they can be coordinated in the context of grief therapy or counseling.

5. Feelings have functions, and should be understood as signals of the state of our meaning making efforts in the wake of challenges to the adequacy of our constructions.

Ironically, despite the emphasis of traditional grief theories on the emotional sequelae of bereavement, affective grief responses are typically treated as merely symptomatic, as problems to be overcome with the passage

of time or the administration of "treatment." In contrast to this characterization of our affective response to loss, constructivists like George Kelly view
emotions as integral to our meaning-making, as expressions of difficult to
observe construing processes. [15] Restated in other terms, *feelings have a function,* and are to be respected as integral to the process of meaning reconstruction, rather than controlled or eliminated as unwanted by-products of
the loss itself or our "dysfunctional" ways of thinking about it.

Drawing on Kelly's personal construct account of emotions as "dimensions of transition," I have found it useful to reconceptualize many of
the emotional experiences commonly associated with bereavement in terms
that link them with the perturbation or restoration of our meaning making
efforts. *Denial* is understood as an individual's inability to assimilate a death
event at a given point in time. One does not have recourse to the structure
necessary to fully perceive the loss or its implications for one's continued
living. Denial therefore represents an attempt to "suspend" the unassimilable
event for a time, until its meaning can be grasped in all of its painful clarity.
Depression can be viewed as a bereaved individual's attempt to restrict his or
her focus to fewer and fewer concerns in order to render the world more
manageable. Like settlers on the American frontier who pulled their wagon
trains into a circle to protect against a potentially hostile world, the depressed
individual can be seen as constricting his or her experiential world to defend
against further potential invalidation, and focus attention on "sifting through"
the multiple meanings of the loss. *Anxiety* represents the awareness that the
death event lies largely outside one's ability to explain, predict, and control.
The fact of death or loss is clearly enough perceived, but we remain only
dimly aware of its unsettling implications for our future lives. *Guilt* stems
from the perception that one has behaved in a way contradicting one's central structures of identity. As such, it is a personal, rather than social ascrip-
tion of culpability for having failed to "live up to" self-imposed standards for
one's role vis-a-vis others. *Hostility* can be viewed as the attempt to force
events to conform to our constructions of them, extorting validational evidence for our failed predictions. In this sense, we hostilely impose our own
interpretations on a death event when we force it to fit with the constructions we held prior to the loss, regardless of its "goodness of fit." And, finally,
threat signals the awareness of impending comprehensive change in core

identity structures. A particular form of death or loss may portend sweeping changes in our most basic sense of who we are.

While this list of definitions of emotional transitions associated with loss is a preliminary one, it can be useful in orienting us to the possible meanings of common feelings and stances that characterize bereavement. For example, Clara's depression can be understood as a form of constriction of her experiential world, to the point that she was preoccupied almost totally with her role in relation to her dying husband. While this focus on his suffering and her unresolved relationship with him was painful, it can also be seen as adaptive, insofar as it allowed her to shift the focus away from other anxiety producing areas of her life—such as the expectations of others and the necessary reorganization of her life in the wake of his eventual death. Clara also contended with a heavy feeling of guilt, as described here, whenever she withdrew even for a day from her core role as a selfless caregiver in relation to Ed. In contrast, Kerry's initial emotional experience during her son's long dying trajectory was one of denial, as she tried vainly to maintain the hope that he would recover and lead a normal life. As the anguishing reality of his condition became apparent, however, she undertook a thorough revision of her meaning system in line with her cosmological explanation of the event, transforming herself and her values in the process While this conceptualization of emotions in meaning-making terms is useful in promoting a fuller understanding of the dynamics of individual cases like these, it has also been helpful in suggesting novel ways of operationalizing death attitudes in research settings, as represented in an extensive program of study on the threat of personal death conducted by personal construct investigators. [16]

6. We construct and reconstruct our identities as survivors of loss in negotiation with others.

Too often, grief theories isolate the bereaved person, focusing so exclusively on the reactions of the individual suffering loss that his or her connection to relevant others is functionally ignored. While I too find that a useful grief theory must account for the personalism of loss, I ultimately believe that adjustment to loss can only be understood in a broader social context. For this reason, "grief work" can be seen as being done at the level of three interdependent and nested systems, corresponding to the self, family, and broader society, respectively.

At the level of the self, I find it more enlightening to view the individual as a constellation or community of semi-autonomous "selves," each of which is supported by certain relationships in the individual's life, and each of which might respond to death or loss in different ways. Adopting a metaphor of the self as a complex system of personalities, coping capacities, beliefs, and so on seems to offer greater clinical utility than traditional theories of personality that suggest or imply a notion of the self as an integrated entity. A more "decentralized" conception of the self, for example, can help sensitize us to the multiple ways in which the "same" individual perceives and responds to a loss, sometimes in conflicting or ambivalent fashion. [17]

At the level of the family, I assume that grieving is a public as well as private act, one whose expression is regulated by norms of family interaction, family roles, hierarchies of power, support, and other features of family structure and process. Even such apparently "private" experiences as remembering the deceased have a collective dimension, as stories told about the family member who has died become part of the "public record" of the deceased person's life, shaping as well as codifying memories and their possible disputation by various family members. [18]

Finally, personal and family responses to loss can be best understood against the backdrop of broader community and cultural interpretations of death and loss, the expectations imposed on bereaved persons, and the norms that regulate the mourning process. At times the influence of the broader society on the grief experience of one of its members is subtle and abstract (as in implicit expectations for how someone of a particular gender, age, or ethnicity will grieve, a topic treated more extensively in the next chapter), while at other times, appropriate grief behavior is systematically delineated. [19] Such cultural and community constructions of particular losses may also be contradictory, as when general societal beliefs recognize the special poignancy of the accidental death of a child, but the local media implicitly blame the parents for "neglectfully" allowing it to happen.

Clara and Kerry's experiences illustrate the interactions of various levels of these systems. The concept of self as a multifaceted entity is most evident in the case of Kerry, who came to sharply delineate a more "extroverted" self seen by the world, and a more "introverted" self experienced in quiet moments of reflection. Much of the transformation experienced across the course of her son's chronic illness and through the bereavement that followed had to do with tapping the resources of this deeper, but quieter voice within her. The impact of family roles, on the other hand, is more striking in the case of Clara, whose long-standing role as the one who gave selflessly to others contributed to painful complications in her relationship to her failing husband. Reciprocally, Ed's angry demandingness in the nursing home, while no longer backed by the threat of physical assault, was consistent with his well established position of power and domination in the family. Clara's son, Richard, also played an important role in her struggle, pushing insistently for her to "cut herself off" from a man who he had seen chronically abuse her. Kerry's family relationships, by contrast, were conspicuous by their absence from her account of her grieving, raising questions about whether any intimate others existed who validated her view of the meaning of her loss or supported her in her quest for a deeper and wiser sense of herself as a woman. Ultimately, for both Clara and Kerry, these personal and family factors were nested within broader societal constructions of the appropriate role of women as caretakers, although the restrictions of this role were more keenly felt by Clara as a function of ethnic expectations as well gender stereotyping.

In summary, the reconstruction of a personal world of meaning in the wake of loss must take into account our ongoing relationships with real and symbolic others, as well as the resources of the mourners themselves. Ultimately, we are faced with the task of transforming our identities so as to redefine our symbolic connection to the deceased while maintaining our relationship with the living. [20] Our attempts to do so may resonate or be dissonant with the views of others such as immediate family or more distant social contacts. To understand even the most private dimensions of loss, we must place them in a social context that supports, opposes, or ignores our experience and need to change. Conflicts or contested meanings in these social contexts contribute to difficulties in adapting to loss, whereas consonance in the multiple social circles that are affected by the loss can support a more coherent revision of our life narratives.

clusion

In this brief chapter I have tried to introduce the outlines of an emerging perspective on grief, one that stands in some contrast to traditional theories that focus on general stages, tasks, or symptoms that are presumed to have relevance to all bereaved persons. Instead, I have tried to place inflection on the extent to which adaptation to loss is shaped by personal, familial, and cultural factors that are too often marginalized in efforts to formalize and standardize our models. In taking this stance, I have suggested that meaning reconstruction is the central process of grieving, and have offered a few preliminary principles for the construction of a more adequate theory compatible with this perspective. Finally, I have tried to illustrate some of the propositions that derive from such a constructivist account of loss by drawing upon the experience of two women who have faced major loss in two of its many forms. But ultimately, this effort is only part of a larger reorientation in grief theory that is underway on the part of clinicians, theorists, and researchers, one that will take some years to coalesce into a more satisfying model. I hope that this book contributes to this trend, and that in its own way it will help advance a richer and more idiographic understanding of loss and its role in human life.

Chapter 7 Research Notes

1. For the sake of readability and focus, I will not digress into an extensive discussion of constructivist theories of knowledge or psychotherapy, which have been treated at great length elsewhere (see Robert Neimeyer and Michael Mahoney (Eds.) (1995). *Constructivism in Psychotherapy.* Washington DC: American Psychological Association). A general framework for understanding constructivism as it relates to grief therapy is provided later in this chapter. However, it may be worth noting at this point that theorists associated with this position reject a view of knowledge as impersonal and objective, science as the collection of facts, and psychotherapy as the expert modification of dysfunctional or unrealistic thoughts, feelings, or behaviors on the part of patients. Instead, human knowing is viewed as deeply individualistic and social, anchored in both personal assumptions and communal agreements that cannot simply be disputed with reference to some "objective" external criterion. Likewise, constructivists approach therapy as a form of intimate collaboration in the exploration of the personal and sometimes problematic meanings with people organize their lives and actions, some of which are amenable to experimentation and renegotiation. While it is beyond the scope of this brief book to detail the several approaches to counseling and psychotherapy that have evolved from this basic constructivist stance, I will allude to several throughout this chapter, and distill some interventions compatible with them that have special relevance for grief counseling.

2. See E. Lindemann, E. (1944). Symptomatology and management of acute grief. *American Journal of Psychiatry, 101,* 141-148.

3. Some indication of the influence of this stagic conception of loss is its virtual hegemony in international medical school curricula on death and dying: Kübler-Ross's model is by far the most common resource (typically the only resource) cited by faculty members teaching residents about adaptation to death and loss. See Barbara Downe-Wambolt and Deborah Tamlyn (1997). An international survey of death education trends in faculties of nursing and medicine. *Death Studies, 21,* 177-188.

4. For a balanced review, see Corr, C. A. (1993). Coping with dying: lessons that we should and should not learn from the work of Elisabeth Kubler-Ross. *Death Studies, 17,* 69-83. An empirically oriented critique of research on these traditional assumptions has been provided by C. Wortman and R. Silver (1989). The myths of coping with loss. *Journal of Consulting and Clinical Psychology, 57,* 349-357.

5. A further sign of rethinking of grief theories long taken for granted is now occurring in psychoanalytic circles. For most of this century, the dominant analytic view has been informed by Freud's description of mourning as a period of desolation following the loss of a significant "object" (e.g., loved one), during which one gradually "works through" the loss by withdrawing emotional energy from the object, so that such energy eventually can be invested in new relationships. Successive generations of analysts have taken this as the cornerstone of their theorizing about loss, presuming that withdrawal from the world and a ruminative preoccupation with thoughts of the deceased were part and parcel of the process. However, George Hagman has recently reviewed both clinical and research evidence that questions virtually every aspect of this psychodynamic conceptualization. Instead of desolation and withdrawal from the world and the image of the lost object, Hagman contends, the bereaved individual normally experiences a sense of being *revitalized* at the point of acknowledging his or her grief, and tends to maintain attachments with both the deceased and other persons. Hagman particularly emphasizes the individuality of grieving, and the need to move beyond descriptions of generic symptomatology to a consideration of less obvious dynamics involved in particular cases. Both emphases are highly compatible with the model being set forth here. See George Hagman (1995), Mourning: A review and reconsideration. *International Journal of Psychoanalysis, 76,* 909-925.

6. Because of its focus on meaning and its frequent deployment in the clinical context, constructivism is sometimes viewed as a variation of cognitive therapy. However, most traditional forms of cognitive therapy are far more objectivistic, regarding meanings as problematic if they depart from presumed norms of "rationality" and correspondence with external "reality."

For this reason, the relationship between these two clinical traditions is complex, leading to quite different forms of practice. For more extended discussion of this point, see R. A. Neimeyer (1993). Constructivism and the cognitive psychotherapies: Some conceptual and strategic contrasts. *Journal of Cognitive Psychotherapy, 7,* 159-171, and R. A. Neimeyer (1998), Cognitive therapy and the narrative trend: A bridge too far? *Journal of Cognitive Psychotherapy, 12,* in press.

7. I am indebted to my colleague Barry Fortner for his assistance in formulating these propositions. Barry, along with Nancy Keesee, has helped extend the meaning reconstruction model and test some of its procedures for assessing the personal ways in which people construe their loss experiences. A preliminary report of this work appears in R. A. Neimeyer, N. J. Keesee & B. V. Fortner (1998). Loss and meaning reconstruction: Propositions and procedures. In S. Rubin, R. Malkinson & E. Wiztum (Eds.). *Traumatic and Non-traumatic loss and bereavement: Clinical theory and practice.* Madison, CT: Psychosocial Press.

8. See C. M. Parkes (1988). Bereavement as a psychosocial transition: Processes of adaptation to change. *Journal of Social Issues, 44,* 53-65.

9. Rando summarizes Parkes' position and that of other prominent grief theorists in her 1995 chapter entitled Grief and mourning: Accommodating to loss. In H. Wass and R. A. Neimeyer (Eds.) *Dying: Facing the facts,* (3rd ed., pp. 211-241). Washington DC.: Taylor & Francis.

10. See M. Braun & D. Berg (1994). Meaning reconstruction in the experience of parental bereavement. *Death Studies, 18,* 105-129, and E. M. Milo (1997). Maternal responses to the life and death of a child with a developmental disability: A story of hope. *Death Studies, 21,* 443-476.

11. See Chapter 1, footnote 5 for an elaboration on this "dual process" model of mourning. The activity of grieving is also discussed in some detail in Chapter 4.

12. Theoretically inclined readers may find Linda Viney's treatment of grieving from a personal construct perspective interesting, insofar as it traces different ways of reaffirming or reorienting one's construct system in the face of loss. See L. L. Viney (1991). The personal construct theory of death and loss: Toward a more individually oriented grief therapy. *Death Studies, 15,* 139-155.

13. For an in-depth discussion of Kerry's case, see R. A. Neimeyer, N.J. Keesee and B. V. Fortner (1998). Loss and meaning reconstruction: Propositions and procedures. In S. Rubin, R. Malkinson & E. Wiztum (Eds.). *Traumatic and Non-traumatic loss and bereavement: Clinical theory and practice.* Madison, CT: Psychosocial Press. In this chapter, my colleagues and I recapitulate the outline of the meaning reconstruction model, but also illustrate several specific constructivist methods for therapeutic assessment and intervention with bereaved persons. Some of these procedures are presented more briefly in the *Personal Applications* section with which this book concludes.

14. This focus on "re-storying" loss is introduced in Chapter 5 of this book; more extensive treatments of narrative approaches and methods in therapy can be found in R. A. Neimeyer, R. A. (1995). Client generated narratives in psychotherapy. In R. A. Neimeyer and M. J. Mahoney (Eds.) *Constructivism in Psychotherapy* (pp. 231-246). Washington DC: American Psychological Association, and Michael White and David Epston(1990). *Narrative means to therapeutic ends.* New York: Norton.

15. Kelly's psychology of personal constructs is concerned centrally with understanding human activity as the attempt to devise workable personal theories with which to organize our understanding of the world, guide our action, and construct role relationships with other people. When our theories are invalidated by unanticipated turns of events, Kelly proposed that we experience a range of painful emotions, which signal the kind of challenge posed to our meaning making efforts. In this section I extrapolate from Kelly's original treatment of these issues to propose phenomenologically grounded definitions of various emotions commonly associated with loss. For Kelly's own thinking, consult George Kelly (1955). *The Psychology of*

Personal Constructs, New York: Norton; reprinted by London: Routledge, in 1991.

16. For a review of this broad empirical literature, see R. A. Neimeyer (1994). The Threat Index and related methods. In R. A. Neimeyer (Ed.) (1994). *Death Anxiety Handbook: Research, Instrumentation, and Application.* Washington DC: Taylor & Francis.

17. This image of the self as multiplistic and coalitional, rather than singular and essential, is coherent with recent social constructionist scholarship emphasizing the ephemerality of identity, which is ultimately anchored in social relationships. For a more expanded theoretical treatment of these issues, as well as some qualifications about the utter abandonment of the concept of selfhood, see Michael Mascolo, Laura Craig-Bray, and Robert Neimeyer (1997). The construction of meaning and action in development and psychotherapy: An epigenetic systems perspective. In G. J. Neimeyer & R. A. Neimeyer (Eds.) *Advances in personal construct theory* (Vol. 4). Greenwich, CN: JAI Press.

18. A particularly poignant illustration of this process of collective remembering has been provided by Gordon Riches and Pamela Dawson, who describe the way in which bereaved parents make use of photos and other memorabilia associated with their deceased children in order to facilitate communication with others about the reality of their lives, and the continued value of their relationship to them. In keeping with the view being advanced in this book, these authors view such shared reminiscence as a way of developing a "story in which past and present relationships are represented and interrogated for meaning." See Gordon Riches and Pamela Dawson (1998), Lost children, living memories: The role of photographs in processes of grief and adjustment among bereaved parents, *Death Studies,* in press.

19. For a lucid description of the tight regulation of mourning experiences within one ethnic tradition, see J. B. Wolowelsky (1996). Communal and individual mourning dynamics within traditional Jewish law. *Death Studies, 20,* 469-480.

20. This point echoes the perspective of Dennis Klass and his colleagues on the role of maintaining symbolic connection to the lost loved one, a topic explored in Chapter 4 (see also Ch. 4, research note 9).

Chapter 8

Dimensions of Diversity in the Reconstruction of Meaning [1]

Bill and Martha sought therapy with me one year to the day after the death of their son, Michael, age 22. From his youth Michael had suffered from a severe and life threatening asthma, from which he died during his junior year abroad at the university. With Bill's stoic support, Martha tearfully described how "everything special about our family died with Michael," leaving them ordinary people, trudging dutifully through ordinary lives, with two other ordinary sons. In part, Michael's "specialness" derived ironically from his illness, because as Martha stated, "having a chronically ill child gives a focus to your life that few other things can." But it soon became evident that Michael's unique role in the family went beyond the intense mutual bond he formed with his devoted mother: he was also the "conduit" for other family members to relate to one another, the bearer of the loftiest ambitions to excel and explore the world, and the one who subscribed to *U.S. News*, *National Geographic*, and *Smithsonian* magazines, and injected their political and cultural sensibilities into the otherwise "local" conversations among family members. Martha's response to his death was to cling tightly to his memory, resisting Bill's insistence on redecorating Michael's room, to the point of wishing that she could "have him encased in glass and lying on his bed" so that she could feel closer to him in his "shrine." In contrast, Bill felt compelled to "make plans for the future," and "find ways to control the kind of thinking that creates depression." Both spouses urgently sought spiritual responses to the unanswerable question of "what made Michael get asthma," and both sought solace through carrying his pens, briefcase, and other cherished possessions. But each ultimately attempted to adapt to the wrenching loss of their son in ways that presented them with very different challenges. While Bill acknowledged the desperate insufficiency of his efforts to "adjust to reality by using the power of positive thinking," Martha conceded that her "refusal to deal with Michael's death prevented her from dealing with his life." Each was feeling increasingly estranged from the other, stuck in a cycle of grieving that seemed unable to move forward. I was left wondering how I could support them as individuals, while simultaneously helping them recover a sense of intimate collaboration in grieving their son's death in ways that seemed irreconcilably opposed.

· · · · · · · · · ·

My only contact with Mayumi, a first generation, 40 year old Japanese American widow, took place in the emergency room of a large metropolitan hospital. Since her husband's apparently accidental shooting death two years earlier, Mayumi had become increasingly depressed and immobilized. Neither the prescription medicines she had come to rely on to dull her pain, nor the offered support of friends and family members compensated for what she had lost, and she described herself as "empty" and "without value." Although she was an intelligent and capable woman, she had become dependent on her eldest son to make decisions about the most minute aspects of her life, even if he ultimately squandered the family's resources on fast cars and needless luxuries, undermining her long-term financial security. Her ER visit was precipitated by a serious suicide attempt through drug overdose, a "failed" act that compounded her shame and sense of "dishonoring" her family. I consistently sensed that Mayumi's manner of coping with her grief expressed her culture as much as her personality, and that her inability to re-engage life in the wake of her loss reflected her traditional conception of widowhood; in Japanese, the term "widow," *miboujin,* is literally translated as *"she who is not yet dead."* This seemed an apt description for her loss of moorings for her identity following her husband's death, so that her own death seemed the only logical solution to her predicament. As I prepared to entrust her inpatient care to a Euro-American male psychiatrist, I worried about how much of her experience as a Japanese American woman would be pathologized (perhaps as a "dependent personality") or missed entirely by the medical establishment, and how she might be further estranged from potential sources of help by the imposition of Western norms for grieving.

· · · · · · · · · ·

If we examine the process of grieving in the concrete particulars of people's lives, we are immediately pushed to the boundaries of popular grief theories, with their simplifying assumptions about stages of emotional adjustment to loss and universal tasks to be mastered by the bereaved individual. Instead, the intimate details of people's stories of loss suggest a complex process of adaptation to a changed reality, a process that is at the same time immensely personal, intricately relational, and inevitably cultural. My goal in this brief chapter is to reflect on these complexities, adopting as our starting point a view of grieving as a process of *meaning reconstruction,* with special emphasis on its diversity rather than sameness across persons and groups. I will therefore review a few basic propositions of the meaning reconstruction model outlined in the previous chapter, and follow this with a consideration of three factors—culture, gender, and spirituality—that contribute to the form and shape of this meaning-making in the lives of those who have lost.

ving as a Process of Meaning Reconstruction

In response to the growing dissatisfaction with traditional models of mourning, a "new wave" of grief theory is emerging, one that is less the product of any particular author than it is the expression of a changed *zeitgeist* about the nature of bereavement as a human experience Among the common elements of these newer models are:

(a) skepticism about the universality of a predictable "emotional trajectory" that leads from psychological disequilibrium to readjustment, coupled with an appreciation of more complex patterns of adaptation,

(b) a shift away from the presumption that successful grieving requires "letting go" of the one who has died, and toward a recognition of the potentially healthy role of maintaining continued symbolic bonds with the deceased,

(c) attention to broadly cognitive processes entailed in mourning, supplementing the traditional focus on the emotional consequences of loss,

(d) greater awareness of the implications of major loss for the bereaved individual's sense of identity, often necessitating deep-going revisions in his or her self-definition,

(e) increased appreciation of the possibility of life-enhancing "post-traumatic growth" as one integrates the lessons of loss, and

(f) broadening the focus of attention to include not only the experience of individual grievers, but also the reciprocal impact of loss on families and broader (sub)cultural groups.

In response to these trends, I have tried to sketch in earlier chapters of this book the outlines of an alternative model of mourning, one that argues that *meaning reconstruction in response to a loss is the central process in grieving.* In keeping with the broader constructivist approach to psychotherapy from which it derives, this approach is informed by a view of human beings as inveterate meaning-makers, weavers of narratives that give thematic significance to the salient plot structure of their lives. Innovating upon culturally available systems of belief, individuals construct permeable, provisional meaning structures that help them interpret experiences, coordinate their relationships with others, and organize their actions toward personally significant goals. Importantly, however, these frameworks of meaning are anchored less in some "objective" reality, than in specific negotiations with intimate others and general systems of cultural discourse. One implication of this social constructionist view is that the themes on which people draw to attribute significance to their lives will be as variegated as the local conversations in which they are engaged, and as complex as the cross-currents of broader belief systems that inform their personal attempts at meaning making. A further implication of this view is that people may feel varying degrees of "authorship" over the narratives of their lives, with some having a sense of deeply personal commitment to their beliefs, values, and choices, while others feel estranged from those beliefs and expectations that they experience as imposed upon them by others in their social networks or by communal ideologies. [2]

In keeping with this general constructivist thesis, loss is viewed as an event that can profoundly perturb one's taken-for-granted constructions about life, sometimes traumatically shaking the very foundations of one's assumptive world. For Mayumi, her husband's violent death not only deprived her of her life partner, but undercut her sense of cosmological balance, in which her life had meaning principally to the extent that it supported and was sustained by his. In the cruel emptiness brought about by his absence, she struggled futilely to find some alternative framework for living, seeking out a dependent relationship on an undependable son, which was nonetheless coherent with her cultural assumptions about the appropriate roles of men and women. Often, the sustaining assumptions that are violated by the death of a loved one are more subtle, functioning as habitual ways of thinking and acting that regulate our daily lives. In the case of Bill and Martha, for example, many of their day-to-day conversations, aspirations, and even disagreements centered on Michael and his "special" involvements, so that his death left them with few workable means of connecting with an anticipated future, with a preferred identity as a family, or with each other.

One of the key deficiencies in traditional models of grieving is their implicit presumption of universality—the idea that all or most bereaved persons respond similarly to loss at an emotional level. In contrast, a meaning reconstruction view emphasizes the subtle nuances of difference in each griever's reaction, so that no two people (even husband and wife, as in the case of Bill and Martha) can be presumed to experience the same grief in response to the "same" loss. Instead, each person is viewed as the constructor of a different phenomenological world and as occupying a different position in relation to broader discourses of culture, gender, and spirituality, as we shall consider in more detail below. This assumption of the radical incommensurability of grieving across persons challenges professional caregivers to approach bereaved individuals from a position of "not knowing" rather than presumed understanding, necessitating means of accessing each bereaved person's unique experience without imposition of "expert" knowledge. [3]

A third feature of a constructivist approach to loss is the conviction that grieving is an active process, however much the bereavement itself was unbidden. While the "choiceless" nature of the loss can leave persons feeling like pawns in the hands of some larger fate, bereavement in fact thrusts survivors into a period of accelerated decision-making. Martha and Bill faced myriad concrete decisions about which of their son's possessions they would keep and share with others, how and whether to redecorate his bedroom, and whether to seek therapy to assist them in reorienting in a world transformed by his loss. At a very basic level, they even confronted the choice of whether to focus their attention either on the loss itself (doing the "grief work" of sorting through the turbulent feelings triggered by his death), or on the restoration of their lives (through a practical focus on adjustments needed to re-engage their occupational and social worlds). Viewing mourning in this way encourages caregivers to assist bereaved individuals in identifying conscious and unconscious choices they confront, and then helping them sift through their options and make difficult decisions.

Finally, as implied by both of the clinical vignettes with which this chapter opened, the reconstructive processes entailed in grieving cannot be understood as taking place within isolated subjectivities divorced from a larger social world. However private our grief, it is necessarily linked with the responses of others, each constraining and enabling the other. This was perhaps most obvious with Bill and Martha, who attempted to remain "in control" to avoid further "burdening" one another. But it was also true of Mayumi, who struggled to find a place for her distinctively Japanese sense of loss in a Euro-American culture that provided her little validation or understanding for her predicament. Ultimately, reconstructing a world of significance in the wake of bereavement is more than a cognitive exercise; it also requires survivors to recruit social support for their changed identities.

Having provided a thumbnail sketch of a meaning reconstruction approach, I will turn to a brief consideration of three dimensions—culture, gender, and spirituality—that contribute in their own ways to the individuality with which people process the significance of losses in their lives. In touching on these three areas, I will draw particularly on recent qualitative research on bereavement, which lends weight to both a meaning reconstruction model and its distinctiveness for different persons and groups. In highlighting qualitative, rather than quantitative research on death and loss, I in no way wish to diminish the important role played by more conventional statistical methods in theory building—indeed, I have vigorously promoted their refinement and extension in a number of other contexts. [4] However, my colleagues and I ultimately recognize that there are aspects of human meaning making that require a closer engagement with the data of experience than statistical procedures permit, and therefore have begun to extend our own research beyond our clinical work to study a broader range of persons struggling to reconstruct their lives in the wake of loss. [5] In citing qualitative studies on the role of culture, spirituality, and gender, I hope to build a bridge between these efforts and our own, although I acknowledge that a thorough review of such research is beyond the scope of this brief chapter. Instead, my intent is merely to point toward the utility of focus groups, grounded theory, narrative analysis, and ethnographic research in enriching our appreciation of the subtlety and range of personal adaptation to loss.

ural Dimensions of Grieving

Of the various dimensions of human experience that contribute to the diversity of meaning reconstruction in response to loss, *culture* is perhaps the most encompassing. Yet because it surrounds us like an atmosphere, providing us with a sustaining communal repertory of interpretations, beliefs, and social roles, its effects on our style of grieving may often be invisible, at least for those who live within the assumptive frame it provides. Its inclusiveness also makes it difficult to tease out its "separate" contributions, distinct from those made by spirituality, gender, and other dimensions that shape our accommodation to loss. Indeed, culture in some sense even subsumes these other dimensions, insofar as gender arrangements may differ markedly in different cultural settings, and a given culture, broadly defined, may offer multiple forms of institutionalized religion that present competing claims regarding the meaning of death in human life.

Cultural contributions to meaning making begin at the rudimentary level of language, which subtly configures our experience of death and bereavement through its structure as well as its content. Indeed, some scholars have held that the tendency in many cultures to speak of the dead as if they have a continuing existence derives from the generalization of linguistic forms adapted to speak of living, present, entities. [6] For example, Martha tended to seek consolation in her stated belief that in death, Michael "was released from the suffering of his asthma," a commonplace remark that nonetheless implied his continued existence as someone who was asthma-free. Even the basic terms in which bereavement is depicted in different languages give a different connotation to the experience; contrast the Spanish translation of grief as "aflicción," affliction, with its implication of passively suffered misfortune and injury from some outside source, with the English term "grieving," with its more internal and potentially active connotation. Such linguistic usages, taken up almost unconsciously by participants in a culture, indirectly configure the meaning of mourning, and even the experience of oneself as a survivor, in ways that are rarely appreciated. This was vividly illustrated in the case of Mayumi, whose designation as a *miboujin* seemed to confer upon her the status of a shadow figure from the point of her husband's death until her own.

At a more concrete level, cultural beliefs and practices concerning death also frame the meanings individuals construct of the loss experience. Braun and Nichols, for example, conducted focus groups of Asian Americans from four distinct cultural groups—Chinese, Japanese, Vietnamese, and Filipino—in order to elucidate the philosophic resources and practical customs with which each group characteristically responded to death, memorialization, suicide, euthanasia, and a variety of related topics. Their results make clear the considerable diversity among these often indiscriminately aggregated cultural groups, as well as the evolving nature of cultural beliefs and practices as successive generations become more assimilated into mainstream American culture. [7]

The focus group members in their study also provided insights that could improve a caregiver's understanding of the cultural frame within which a bereaved person is seeking to adjust to loss. For example, as a first-generation Japanese American, Mayumi's inability to organize an appropriate Buddhist *pillow sutra* for her husband given the tragic circumstances of his death contributed to her sense of guilt, and may have complicated her grieving by denying her a supportive role in the journey of his soul from this life to the next. [8] Moreover, the generally compassionate and permissive Japanese attitude toward suicide could have made this seem like a nobler and less "pathological" response to her situation than it may have been for a Euro-American facing a similar crisis.

Finally, in addition to recognizing the role of subcultural and ethnic factors in death, dying, and bereavement, [9] it is important to acknowledge the role of popular culture in shaping both our private grief, and our collective response to public losses. The latter was exemplified by the incredible outpouring of public grief over the loss of Princess Diana of Wales, whose tragic death in an automobile accident in September of 1997 triggered shock, outrage, and sadness on the part of millions of persons throughout the world. The subsequent funeral procession, memorial ceremonies, speeches, and media coverage also provided a powerful example of the healing power of public recognition of pain, and fostered greater awareness of our shared need to make sense of a senseless death, and to memorialize the life it ended.

tual Dimensions of Grieving

Like culture, from which it can be only inexactly distinguished, religious and cosmological beliefs can play a profound role in our response to death and loss. Indeed, theorists such as Becker [10] have suggested that a primary function of religion is to help contain our terror of death by providing an interpretive frame within which it can be viewed. In traditional religions like orthodox Judaism, this frame can extend to the prescription of elaborate rituals of mourning for both the bereaved individual and the community, effectively conferring on mourners "pre-packaged" temporary identities that sustain them through the role transition instigated by loss. [11]

As a constructivist, I am especially interested in the ways in which individuals selectively appropriate religious themes that have personal significance, in the process of configuring a spirituality that might or might not resemble the formal religion in which they were raised. As was true with Bill and Martha, who sought answers to the urgent but elusive question of why Michael had to be born with a life-threatening illness, many persons are forced to re-examine their personal spirituality at the point of profound loss. Braun and Berg conducted a grounded theory analysis of this experience, by carefully interviewing ten bereaved mothers and then coding their responses according to emergent themes. They identified three distinct phases of meaning reconstruction—discontinuity, disorientation, and adjustment—and found that the majority of the mothers reinterpreted the meaning structures they held prior to their child's death in order to give it significance. One of their more provocative findings was that those women who could not "place" the loss of their child within their pre-existing framework of spiritual beliefs had greater difficulty adjusting to the loss, whereas those who could assimilate the death as orderly or divinely ordained fared better in the wake of the loss. [12]

Elizabeth Moulton Milo's research on the experience of bereaved mothers of developmentally disabled children adds detail to this depiction of the meaning reconstruction process. [13] Complementing a standardized quantitative grief assessment with intensive, semi-structured interviews, she found that these mothers groped their way toward several different explanations in order to find a special meaning for the life and death of their children. For example, several of the mothers spoke of the child's birth and death as purposeful, intended by God to foster the mother's spiritual growth, a theme also identified in our own case study of Kerry, the mother of a young boy with congenital heart problems. [14] Other participants in Milo's study found meaning through less obviously spiritual, but deeply personal strategies, including the orchestration of a "beautiful," peaceful, or intimate death for their child, resorting to "downward comparisons" to families still less fortunate, or even having recourse to a grim sense of humor. Like Braun and Berg, Milo also found that mothers who could incorporate their child's disability and death into their pre-existing beliefs adapted to these losses more readily. Importantly, however, these constructions were not necessarily cosmic in their meaning; they could as easily express a deeply held secular philosophy of life. For example, one mother who was a social activist had accepted as a "given" that the world was imperfect, that everyone had pain their lives, and that one's task was to ameliorate it whenever possible through involvement and advocacy. A similar range of conventional and unconventional philosophical schemas were noted by Richards and Folkman, in their qualitative analysis of the spiritual themes in interviews with gay men whose partners had died of AIDS. [15] Thus, the process of personal reconstruction following a loss can be facilitated by having recourse to humanistic as well as explicitly theistic beliefs, underscoring the need to respect the individuality of meaning making for each survivor.

ler Roles in Grieving

In an attempt to emphasize the relational context of loss, family theorists sometimes speak of "family grief," or the violation of a "family's assumptions" when confronted with the death of one of its members. Yet, constructivists like Kathleen Gilbert have reminded us that families, per se, do not grieve, hold beliefs, etc.—only individuals do. This implies that different family members may react quite differently to the "same" objective loss, as a function of the different meanings they attach to it, their differing positions in relation to the deceased, their respective roles in the family, and, most relevantly for the present discussion, gender differences in grieving. [16]

Traditional grief theories have been founded on the experiences of bereaved women, and hence have emphasized a "feminine" style as the "healthy" way of responding to loss. From this perspective, theorists and clinicians have stressed the value of emotional expression and self-disclosure, and have typically distrusted "intellectualization" and coping with grief through immersion in activities rather than the seeking of social support. Yet, as Terry Martin and Ken Doka point out, this may amount to little more than a prejudice against "masculine" styles of grieving, in which thinking often precedes feeling, and active problem-solving takes the place of discussion of feelings with others. [17] In the present case examples, this difference in grieving style was illustrated by Bill and Martha, who attempted to give meaning to Michael's life and death in ways that were only partially overlapping. Martha's response to her son's death was to attempt to foster an intense affective sense of his presence by "spending time with him" in his carefully preserved bedroom, frequently visiting his grave, and sharing her tears and feelings openly with others. For his part, Bill was more self-controlled and reserved, voicing only mild "irritation" about his son's need to "push away from all authority figures" as he sought adult independence from his father's guidance. To a greater extent than his wife, Bill also tried to confront and solve the practical problems engendered by his son's death, including the disposition of his property. Despite their shared sadness, Martha and Bill's divergent styles complicated their mourning, as Bill felt distressed and helpless in the face of his wife's seemingly endless pain, and she questioned his empathy for her and his love for Michael in his abrupt attempt to reorganize their lives. Their differing needs also complicated our counseling, which ultimately took the form of separate cognitive therapy for Bill, and more metaphoric, evocative exploration for Martha, before bringing them back together for joint sessions. Such flexibility in grief therapy may be essential to meet the needs of bereaved persons who mourn in a masculine or feminine style, whatever their biological sex.

In addition to considering these broad distinctions in coping styles associated with gender, it is important to examine the specific meanings attached by partners to their ongoing relationship in the wake of loss. Annalies Hagemeister and Paul Rosenblatt have contributed a poignant account of this aspect of meaning reconstruction in their grounded theory analysis of twenty-four couples, two thirds of whom reported a significant break or decline in their sexual relationship following the death of a child. What proved critical in accounting for changes in their sexual contact were the (sometimes discrepant) meanings attached to intercourse by the couple. For example, a number of the spouses acknowledged that they avoided intercourse for a long time after the death because it symbolized how the child had been made, while others withdrew from sexual contact because it signified pleasure, which seemed incompatible with mourning. Still others sought out intercourse specifically because it meant "another chance" to have children, or because it represented a reaffirmation of the relationship and reconnection to life. Significantly, husbands and wives consistently differed in some of the meanings attached to sex, with men more often experiencing physical intimacy as a source of comfort and connection, whereas women were more apt to interpret their partner's advances as intrusive or selfish. [18] This pattern was also evident for Bill and Martha, as he complained of feeling "cut off from her as well as Michael," while she felt he was placing unfair sexual demands on her when she had "nothing more to give." These discrepancies deserve attention in the counseling context, as they can contribute to the pursuit of extramarital affairs in an effort to "feel wanted" by someone, or escape the problematic meanings associated with sexual contact with one's spouse.

Finally, it bears emphasis that culturally prescribed gender roles can be experienced as oppressive or constraining by both sexes. In our case illustrations, this was most evident in the passive and dependent script for widowhood offered to Mayumi, but it can apply equally to European expectations for strength and stoicism on the part of male grievers, who may disregard or suppress aspects of their own reactions in order to comply with these role requirements. Thus, the extent of "match" between gender expectations and personal predilections is important to assess in the course of grief counseling.

ractions and Conclusions

While I have focused on the separate impact of culture, spirituality, and gender, it is worth noting that meaning reconstruction following a loss is made more complex and idiosyncratic not only by the above dimensions of diversity, but also by interactions among them. For example, in the earlier case study of "Kerry" (see Chapter 7), whose two-year old son eventually succumbed to congenital heart problems, her grief was shaped in part by the ambivalent spiritual significance it had for her. Jacob's death, for her, represented not only a cherished opportunity to develop a depth of character for which she yearned, but also a stern attempt by a patriarchal god to break a "matrilineal pattern of female unconsciousness" represented by her mother and herself, before this pattern was passed on to her surviving daughter. Thus, Kerry's deeply personal cosmology represented the confluence of a spiritual quest for meaning in her son's death, and a gendered conception of a somewhat retributive male deity that was deeply inscribed in her culture. Likewise, the interaction of cultural expectations, gender roles, and spiritual beliefs presented distinctive challenges for Mayumi's post-bereavement meaning reconstruction, particularly in an alien American setting that offered few compensatory means of support other than readily available medication. Thus, understanding the unique predicament of individual grievers requires caregivers to tease out the many threads of personal and social construction that are woven together to make up any given person's tapestry of loss.

In closing, a meaning reconstruction view is based on the conviction that grieving persons are active agents in negotiating the course of their post-bereavement adjustment, whether such dimensions as culture, spirituality, and gender seem to facilitate or impede their attempts at reconstructing a life worth living. Ultimately, such broad dimensions serve as forms of socially available discourse offering myriad potential meanings of loss, upon which individuals selectively draw as they configure a new sense of self appropriate to their changed world. I hope that this book contributes in its own way to the efforts of many theorists and investigators to deepen our understanding of this process, and the factors that contribute to its richness and diversity for different persons and groups.

pter 8 Research Notes

1. An earlier version of this chapter was written with the assistance of Nancy Keesee, whose personal courage in articulating the significance of her own losses has been a source of inspiration in the development of the meaning reconstruction model.

2. For an extended discussion of the role of "dominant narratives" in the lives of persons, and psychotherapeutic methods of resisting them, see Gerald Monk and his colleagues (1997). *Narrative therapy in practice*. San Francisco: Jossey Bass.

3. The conceptualization of the therapist's stance from a position of "not knowing" is developed by Harlene Anderson and Harry Goolishian (1992). The client is the expert. In S. McNamee & K. J. Gergen (Eds.), *Therapy as social construction*. Newbury Park, CA: Sage. The most sophisticated expression of the adoption of a non-expert role in the literature on grief in families is Janice Nadeau's highly original 1997 book, *Families making sense of death*. Newbury Park, CA: Sage. Nadeau's use of qualitative research methods to bring to light the subtle and varied ways in which different families accommodate to loss through their conversational meaning making should be required reading for those professionals interested in the position being advanced in this book.

4. I have been most vocal in advocating greater methodological sophistication in the vast and checkered literature on death anxiety and related attitudes, which could benefit from a number of psychometric and statistical refinements. See especially R. A. Neimeyer (Ed.). (1994). *Death anxiety handbook: Research, instrumentation, and application*. New York: Taylor & Francis; and R. A. Neimeyer(1998). Death anxiety research: The state of the art. *Omega, 36*, 89-112.

5. A preliminary report of this work appears in R. A. Neimeyer, N. J. Keesee & B. V. Fortner (1998). Loss and meaning reconstruction: Propositions and procedures. In S. Rubin, R. Malkinson & E. Wiztum (Eds.). *Trau-*

matic and Non-traumatic loss and bereavement: Clinical theory and practice. Madison, CT: Psychosocial Press.

6. A fascinating presentation of this thesis can be found in B. Haussaman (1998). Death and syntax. *Death Studies, 22,* in press. Arthur Zucker provides a philosophic counterpoint to Haussaman's argument in a response article in that same journal issue.

7. See K. L. Braun and R. Nichols (1997). Death and dying in four Asian American cultures. *Death Studies, 21,* 327-359.

8. For a culturally sensitive anthropological depiction of this ritual in a Tibetan context, consult R. E. Goss and D. Klass, D. (1997). Tibetan Buddhism and the resolution of grief. *Death Studies, 21,* 377-396.

9. Readers interested in gaining a vicarious experience of the diversity of ethnic traditions surrounding death are encouraged to see Annette Dula's moving portrayal of the life and death of an elderly black woman in the rural south: A. Dula (1997). The story of Miss Mildred. In K. Doka (Ed.), *Living with grief: When illness is prolonged,* Washington, D. C.: Hospice Foundation of America.

10. E. Becker (1973). *The denial of death.* New York: Macmillan.

11. See Chapter 7, Research Note 19.

12. M. L. Braun and D. H. Berg (1994). Meaning reconstruction in the experience of bereavement. *Death Studies, 18,* 105-129.

13. E. M. Milo (1997). Maternal responses to the life and death of a child with developmental disability. *Death Studies, 21,* 443-476.

14. R. A. Neimeyer, N. J. Keesee and B. V. Fortner (1998). Loss and meaning reconstruction: Propositions and procedures. In S. Rubin, Malkinson, R. & Wiztum, E. (Ed.), *Traumatic and non-traumatic loss and*

bereavement. Madison, CT: Psychosocial Press. A briefer depiction of this case is offered in Chapter 7 of this book.

15. See T. A. Richards and S. Folkman (1997). Spiritual aspects of loss at the time of a partner's death from AIDS. *Death Studies, 21*, 515-540.

16. K. R. Gilbert (1996). "We've had the same loss, why don't we have the same grief?" Loss and differential grief in families. *Death Studies, 20*, 269-284.

17. For an extended discussion, and for practical advice on how to help "masculine" grievers—whether male or female—see T. Martin & K. Doka (1996). Masculine grief. In K. Doka (Ed.), *Living with grief after sudden loss*, (pp. 161-172). Washington, DC: Hospice Foundation of America.

18. A. K. Hagemeister and P. C. Rosenblatt (1997). Grief and the sexual relationship of couples who have experienced a child's death. *Death Studies, 21*, 231-251.

Part 3:

Personal Resources

Chapter 9

Personal Applications

As I was writing the foregoing pages, I hoped that the brief, focused chapters in Part 1 would shed light on the personal experience of grieving, whether the circumstance that occasioned it was the death of a loved one, relationship dissolution, or job loss. I further hoped that the somewhat longer and more theoretical chapters comprising Part 2 would provide conceptual scaffolding for a view of grieving as a process of meaning reconstruction, developing the earlier forays into this domain encountered in Part 1 in chapters on rituals and relationships. But although this material is intended to provide a measure of understanding to both bereaved individuals and those who attempt to help them, I ultimately realize that grieving is a more active process than reading alone implies. For this reason, in the present chapter I will offer several specific applications of some of the ideas developed throughout the book, each of which has proven helpful to bereaved individuals with whom I have worked in grief counseling. Used judiciously, the exercises that follow can help with the task of taking perspective on the losses of our lives, and moving forward with our grieving. However, it is worth emphasizing that techniques in themselves do nothing for the user; it is more a question of what the user does with the techniques offered. Thus, I trust that the reader ultimately will be in the best position to decide how and when to draw selectively on these suggestions, not with the goal of somehow "curing" grief, but instead with the intent of mining its nuances, and mobilizing his or her own healing resources.

How to Use These Exercises

I have found the exercises or applications that follow to be helpful under one of two circumstances, either as *self-help techniques* for coming to terms with one's loss, or as *counselor-offered homework* to support an ongoing course of grief therapy. Because most of these suggestions could easily be adapted to either purpose, I intentionally have not attempted to subdivide these into two separate headings, but instead have offered them together as a repertory of ideas to enrich personal reflection or mobilize relevant action in either context. However, let me offer a few general suggestions at the outset as to how a bereaved individual or grief counselor might use these applications to best advantage. Afterwards, in conjunction with each exercise, I will offer some specific ideas about how it might best be used to facilitate independent personal exploration or guided reconstruction in the context of grief therapy.

Bereaved individuals might browse through the applications that follow, looking for one or more that seem personally relevant to the character and phase of their own grief. In my own use of these applications, either personally or with bereaved clients, I have found them to produce more comfort than conflict, but I urge readers to use discretion about what feels appropriate for them. For example, the idea of constructing a "photo gallery" commemorating the life of someone you have loved and lost can ultimately give a sense of "wholeness" to the life he or she led, as well as acknowledge that person's role in your own. However, many grievers will understandably find that the process of sorting through and organizing such photographs will bring to light bittersweet memories, as I did a few years ago when I compiled a photo album of our family's life prior to my father's death when I was 11. In itself, the pain triggered by such work is neither positive or negative— it is the sense made of the pain, what we do with it, that makes the experience constructive or destructive. My advice is simply to *trust yourself,* and if any given exercise seems either overwhelming or ill-fitting, then set it aside, at least for the time being, if not altogether. As I have repeatedly emphasized in the foregoing pages, there is no one "right way" to grieve, and nothing in this chapter is intended to be prescriptive about what is best for you. This being said, I trust that you will find some of the following activities helpful in coming to terms with your own loss, perhaps through stimulating ideas of your own, beyond the suggestions offered. But remember that not all grief needs to be borne alone, and that there are times when seeking the counsel of a friend, family member, or even a professional counselor may be appropriate. Some recommendations regarding the limits of self-help were offered in Chapter 1.

Grief counselors may find the following personal applications helpful, as I have, in taking an "inventory" of their own grief histories, as a precondition to entering the experiential worlds of their clients. Unlike some of the relatively esoteric "disorders" or problems about which professionals learn in the course of their training, grief is a universal experience, and therefore is the one challenge that we are guaranteed to confront personally as well as professionally. Having a clearer sense of the way we have accommodated to losses in our own lives, as well as the limitations in these modes of accommodation, can help us separate our own issues and answers from those of our clients. Only after attending to our own losses can we stand close enough to the client's experience to sense his or her unique struggle, and yet recognize that it is not our own.

A second use of these exercises is as between-session "homework" in the course of grief therapy. As with all forms of therapy, the work of grief counseling ultimately must transcend the boundaries of the consulting room if it is to have an impact on our clients' lives. Making judicious suggestions about how clients might facilitate their own "grief work" between meetings can help achieve this goal. However, to be used appropriately, these personal applications should be offered to the client with the following guidelines in mind:

1. *Develop a collaborative attitude.* The most useful homework assignments are likely to be mutually designed, rather than therapist assigned. For example, it may be more helpful after a session to ask, "What might you do this week to help you move forward with your grieving/memorialize your son/open a discussion with someone you trust about what concerns you?" than to say, "This week I want you to do..." Of course, any of the ideas sketched below can be offered in a provisional way, especially if grafted onto the important emotional themes that have dominated the preceding session. For instance, a woman who has begun to allude to a barely permissible resent-

ment toward the emotionally domineering husband from whom she was "freed" by a fatal accident might be asked, "How would you feel about writing a private letter to him this week, expressing to him some of the mixed feelings you have in the aftermath of his death? Does this feel like a safe time to do that, or would that still trigger more upsetness or guilt than you could tolerate at this point? What do you think of the idea?" Adopting a genuinely collaborative stance also implies a readiness to modify the homework in light of the client's feedback, or suspend it altogether. All of the exercises below suggest variations that permit you to adapt the application to the client's unique circumstances, but the range of permissible variation is really limited only by your creativity as a therapeutic team and your client's specific needs and resources.

2. *Respect the client's resistance.* If the client balks at a particular suggestion, assume that it is for good reason. What might he or she be experiencing that you have incompletely understood? Might more be "at stake" in the completion of a given activity than you have realized from an "outsider" perspective? One example of this arose in my group therapy with Susan, whose child had died nearly eight years before of SIDS. Group members had begun to challenge what they regarded as her dysfunctional sense of guilt, and urged her to write down and dispute the stream of damning self-accusations that would come to mind whenever she thought of the death. But Susan was quite unable to act on this well-intended advice, until we identified the source of her resistance: holding on to her guilt, for her, represented the ultimate proof that she was a "good mother," despite her child's unfortunate death. Once she was able to envision some alternative means of cultivating a continued connection to his memory, she was able gradually to relinquish her guilt, and with it the depression that had blocked her from full involvement with her surviving children.

Just as it can be helpful to inquire into complete blockages in beginning assignments, as in the case of Susan, it is helpful to process problems that arise in the course of partially completing an assignment. For example, in the earlier illustration of writing a letter to someone with whom the client had an ambivalent relationship, the counselor could inquire about specific points in the letter at which the client bogged down, became overwhelmed with anger, or suddenly "forgot" where she was heading. If respectfully understood rather than disrespectfully overridden, such "resistance" can be "grist for the mill" of therapeutic discussion, and yield rich insights into the client's accommodation to loss.

3. *Respect the client's privacy.* Allow clients to "edit" what they produce in response to any given exercise, sharing with you only what they choose. For example, after inquiring how a particular assignment went, you might ask, "Is there any part of that you'd like us to concentrate on today? Is there any part you would prefer to keep private?" If clients feel free to reserve personal reactions without feeling pressured to share them immediately with others, they are more likely to use the exercises in an uncensored fashion to sort through issues and reactions that they fear would be embarrassing or shameful. Acknowledging such reactions fully to themselves may then serve as a step toward disclosing them to others.

4. *Integrate homework into the session.* Be sure to make a note following each session about any initiatives the client has committed to undertake prior to your next meeting, and begin the next session by inquiring about how the assignment went. Failure to mention the homework quickly conveys the impression that it is trivial and expendable, whereas showing curiosity about the process and product of homework completion drives home the point that it is integral to therapy.

I have found it most helpful to fully integrate between-session work by asking clients to read, or in some other way, actively share the results of exercises with me, as opposed to simply handing me a sheet with their responses written out. In the latter case, the counselor is faced with two bad options— either to set the assignment aside for later reading and discussion, thereby missing the opportunity for immediate feedback, or to read it silently in session, while the client anxiously awaits the counselor's response. If the client is encouraged to read it aloud, on the other hand, he or she can discretely "edit" it in the course of reading, or pause to discuss a particular aspect of the application in greater detail. On the rare occasion when a client is too reticent to share his or her reactions in this way, I ask permission to read it aloud slowly and with feeling, pausing to share my own reactions and encourage therapeutic discussion of the results. Doing this sensitively can help build a bridge between client and therapist, and facilitate direct client sharing in later sessions.

5. *Recognize the value of "being," as well as "doing."* As a final note, my endorsement of an active model of grieving should not be taken as advocacy for an overly "busy" approach to therapy, one that attempts to hurry a client's processing of a loss with the goal of promptly ameliorating distress and returning to a presumed emotional equilibrium. Grieving takes time, and there will be many points in the process of grief therapy when no assignments or actions are indicated, beyond attending to what is taking shape in one's life, or even disattending from the loss altogether in order to devote one's energies elsewhere. On average, I find that my clients and I are drawn toward the use of some form of between-session work in perhaps one third of our sessions, and I am more likely to suggest one of the following applications when the loss has in some way become the focus of later problems in the client's life (e.g., feeding into a fear of abandonment in other close relationships). Even in such cases, these applications are designed to promote as much reflection as action, fostering a balance between the "internal" dimension of grief work and the "external" process of adjusting to a world transformed by the loss.

A related point concerns the predominantly "narrative" nature of the applications that follow, as many of them use some form of personal writing to promote reflection upon and integration of loss. I confess that this expresses my own interests and predilections toward narrative and constructivist forms of therapy, [1] and acknowledge that not all grieving persons are drawn to "work through" their grief with pencil and paper. Still, I have often been surprised at the contribution of several of these methods to the grief work of less highly verbal individuals—indeed, a well-chosen narrative method (e.g., a short and to-the-point unsent letter) may prove to be a powerful means of articulating and addressing loss in such cases precisely *because* written self-expression is a novel experience. If counselors and bereaved persons can drop the bias that writing and reflection are the sole prerogatives of highly literate people, they may be surprised by the simple eloquence of which the majority of grieving people are capable, if given encouragement to express old concerns in fresh ways.

Nonetheless, I do not consider a narrative approach to self-change to be limited to the written word, and hence have suggested several imaginal, practical, and conversational applications and variations that are intended to speak to those who process experience in different ways. I hope that readers of this book will experiment with a wide range of these applications, to discover what works best for them and those they attempt to help.

In closing, the keys to intelligent use of the following applications, whether adopted as self-help strategies by the bereaved individual or therapeutic assignments by the grief counselor, are appropriateness, flexibility, and creativity. I hope that you will find some ideas here that will contribute to your efforts, and I invite you to share with me additional exercises that you discover or invent that extend the range of the exercises that follow. To reach me, simply write:

Robert A. Neimeyer, Ph.D.
Department of Psychology
University of Memphis
Memphis, TN 38152-6400
e-mail: neimeyer@cc.memphis.edu

Applications

The personal applications that follow are grouped alphabetically, but this in no way implies that the exercises should be used in any particular sequence. For example, counselors may find it valuable to begin a course of grief therapy with some form of the *Meaning Reconstruction Interview*, while bereaved individuals who are well into their grieving process may feel that beginning a *Memory Book* on their loved one is an appropriate next step in gaining perspective. In each case, I have described (1) *indications* of when, with what sorts of issues, and in what sort of settings a particular application may be most useful, (2) *variations* on the basic application that increase its scope and relevance to particular grievers, and (3) *precautions* about its potential drawbacks or limitations, especially if misapplied. When illustrations of a given technique seemed as if they would help convey its use in practice, I have also provided actual examples derived from my personal experience with them in grief therapies I have conducted or in my own life. Finally, when the structure of the application was conducive to it, I have left some blank space following the exercise, so that bereaved individuals who wish to use this section as a workbook can note their responses directly on the pages that follow for convenience and later reference.

Biographies

Indications: One traditional technique for honoring the lives of important people is the biography, a written record that provides an account of the significant events, persons, places, and projects that shaped the subject's life. As a tool for gaining perspective on a loss, it can also serve the psychological function of allowing us to take stock of the whole of our loved one's life, to appreciate its complexities and contradictions, and especially its impact on our own. While there is no single way to approach the task of recording a loved one's life story—just as there is no single style for writing historical biographies—a few general pointers follow:

1. *Consider the source.* What kind of "research" do you want to do to support your writing? Biographies can be written from a first person point of view ("My Memories of ....."), or they can draw upon the shared recollections of several relatives or friends. Likewise, they can be based solely upon interviews, or can incorporate "objective data" (such as official documents, letters, newspaper stories, and so on) that can help provide a structure for the more impressionistic accounts contributed by living persons. Each approach is defensible, but each also leads to a different kind of product.

2. *Look for the surprises.* Especially if you draw on the views of several sources, welcome points of disagreement, or differing opinions or recollections that uncover aspects of the subject that may not fit your initial image of who he or she was.

3. *Know your limits.* Any life, if examined closely, can yield so many observations, interpretations, and explanations that even the most ambitious chronicle could not contain them. Indeed, some years ago, an entire book was written on the topic of one boy's day! So reconcile yourself to telling an incomplete story, comforted by the recognition that even a one-page obituary is more than is done to recognize most people's lives. Your story does not have to be exhaustive to carry meaning for you, and perhaps others.

4. *Use the facts, but don't be enslaved by them.* While it is usually valuable to anchor the biography in important dates, jobs, living circumstances, and so on of the subject, don't be afraid to go beyond these to discuss the more ambiguous, but interesting conjectures about your subject's motives, goals, and struggles. Try to answer the question: What do these public

facts, statements, and commitments say about the private person behind them?

5. *Write for your audience.* Any form of writing can be addressed to different readerships, and it is usually helpful to have your audience in mind before setting pencil to paper or finger to keyboard. On the one hand, you may choose to write solely for yourself, in effect making the biography a sort of extended entry in your personal journal. On the other extreme, you could write for a general readership, in some cases even seeking actual publication of the resulting manuscript (an option usually open only to professional writers addressing famous subjects). In between these two extremes are a host of audiences—one's spouse, when writing the brief story of a child who died, or a larger group of relatives sharing an interest in a parent or grandparent. Obviously, different readers are likely to have varying amounts of background understanding of the subject of the biography, different levels of interest in the particulars of his or her life, and varying degrees of receptivity to your personal impressions or feelings in interpreting or embellishing the story. In general, a biography that is tilted toward the personal feelings of the author should be disseminated to a wide readership only with caution.

Example: Carol's relationship to her father had always been a complex one. On the one hand, he seemed to be her protector, the one person who loved her unconditionally, and who defended her from the criticisms of her mother and older sister. On the other hand, in her adult life she had begun to have strange dreams and disturbing, if ambiguous memories of early interactions with him, which to her suggested that he also may have sexually abused her. In therapy with me, she recalled withdrawing from him in adolescence when she joined a Christian religious cult, which enforced a "no contact" code with family as a supposed prerequisite to devoting oneself to one's "mission." It was during her years of immersion in this sect that her father developed cancer and rapidly declined, while Carol kept her distance as demanded by the charismatic leaders of the group. If she only remained true to her mission and had enough faith, she was told, her father would live, whereas if she doubted and returned to see him, he would surely die. Her father's inevitable death therefore triggered both a crisis of belief for Carol and a wave of guilt, which reinforced her sense of foundationlessness and self-hatred as she moved into adult life.

In the context of therapy, Carol felt compelled to reopen the thorny issue of her relationship with her father, which seemed to have so complicated her relationships with men in general. As part of this effort, she made a four day trip to the small town where she was raised, and spoke to a number of older surviving relatives and friends of her father about their recollections of him, and of their family life during her early years. In addition, she wrote her brother and sister and invited them to contribute their own memories and interpretations of their childhood, phoning them periodically to consult about the emerging story of who her father was, as a husband, parent, worker, and man. The resulting chronicle began to support the possible reality of her early abuse, while also disclosing sides of her father's personality and concerns that had been invisible to her in childhood. In the face of these complexities and contradictions, Carol decided not to strive for a single coherent story, but instead to collect together the multiple stories, and share a copy with each person who contributed, and who was interested in seeing a copy. Despite the lack of clear resolution of their relationship, Carol felt that the process of constructing her father's biography served many useful purposes, including stimulating personal memories that then became "grist for the mill" of her therapy, honoring those parts of their relationship that were genuinely good and supportive, validating some of her suspicions regarding those aspects that were not, and permitting her to see both her father's life and her own as ongoing stories that continued to develop in unexpected directions, rather than something that was static or frozen in time. Just as important, becoming her father's unofficial biographer opened Carol to the confidences of many other family members, revitalizing her relationships with her previously estranged brother and sister, and aunts and uncles. While much work remained to be done to make her own life story a more satisfying one, writing her father's biography allowed her to envision future chapters of her own life story that were not mere reiterations of the past. [2]

Variations: Not all biographies need to be major projects, and not all need to be triggered by crises or conflicts in our relationships with those we have lost. For example, Gloria unambivalently loved her father, and her sole regret was not being able to say a final "good-bye" to him during his last hospitalization. But she took delight in collecting stories of her father told by his friends and coworkers, and enjoyed passing them on to her daughter, who was very young when he died. For her, collecting reminiscences of her father connected her to his memory, and was part of an oral tradition of storytelling in her family in which she proudly took part.

Not all biographies need to be written. Just as Gloria served as an informal biographer without pen and paper, it is possible to record our own recollections and those of others using a tape recorder or video camera, a variation that has the added advantage of capturing something of the personalities of the storytellers, as well as the subject of their stories.

Finally, not all biographies need to be about other people. Especially when we are trying to gain perspective on the overall legacy of several losses in our lives, it may be helpful to write a brief *autobiography,* as viewed from the vantage point of the present. If this process seems too daunting, even the attempt to draft chapter headings that organize and punctuate the flow of our life can be quite provocative. For example, I recently constructed the following chapter headings to scaffold my own life story (with a note about chapter contents in parentheses after each), but with no real plan to ever develop it into a full autobiography.

I. The Romance of Memory
   (idyllic childhood recollections, more complex realities)
II. Childhood's End
   (our father's death, move to Florida)
III. The Crucible
   (adolescent struggles and love relationships)
IV. Breaking Free
   (move to college, building a life of my own)
V. A Study in Contrast
   (philosophical investments, personal projects)
VI. The Trouble with Being Earnest
   (the invisible constraints of intense involvement)
VII. The Way of the Cat
   (resistance against an authoritarian work setting)
VIII. The Bee Hive
   (building a "research empire," struggles with overcommitment)

IX. In a Family Way
   (seeking balanced investments in work and home life)
X. Broadening Horizons
   (preserving core values, extending old boundaries)

Obviously, there is no preferred way to organize one's autobiography—except according to one's own preferences! But the chapter titles that we concoct to do so speak volumes about the important themes we winnow from our experiences, the way we structure the past, construe the present, and anticipate the future. Such an exercise can become a jump off point for other forms of reflective writing (e.g., journal work), or can be a source of rich discussion in the context of personal counseling or family conversations.[3]

Precautions: Like most of the applications described in this chapter, biographies can be unsettling to the same extent that they are powerful. While the attempt to capture on paper a few of the objective facts of our subject's life can be helpful (e.g., as a way of preserving information on births, deaths, etc. for future generations), an objective chronology is also less helpful as a tool for personal growth or therapeutic exploration. On the other extreme, a deep and probing inquiry into either the life of a loved one or our own can be threatening, liberating, and strangely moving, both to ourselves as authors and to other readers with whom we choose to share it. Thus, it is important to consider your level of vulnerability before undertaking a task that may turn out to be as unsettling as it can be healing.

A second precaution concerns what might be entitled the "realist fallacy:" the idea that we will somehow reach the truth, the whole truth, and nothing but the truth about our subject's life. While we may each have a sense of what feels honest and dishonest to report as "fact," writing a biography will soon make clear that reality is a social construction, which looks very different from the vantage point of different observers. For this reason, it is important to not try to wrap up our story too neatly, striving to cover or "smooth" the inconsistencies that inevitably arise. In contrast, one might view the telling of any story as an invitation (to ourselves and others) to retell it from a different vantage point, a process that might allow very different observations to emerge.

Drawing and Painting

Indications: While the spoken or written word has great power in helping us come to terms with loss, by no means does it have an exclusive role in the reconstruction of meaning. For many persons, young and old, symbolic drawing or other forms of artistic expression can be equally significant in articulating the losses they have suffered, and the possibilities they envision for their future. [4] When used as part of a personal journal or grief counseling, the resulting depictions can also be interrogated for their nuances of meaning, often providing a bridge into feelings and issues that are difficult to speak to in a more direct fashion.

Example: Josh was 19 when Jennifer left him for someone else, triggering a depressive spiral that left him wondering whether life was truly worth living. As part of his group therapy, I encouraged Josh and other group members to "draw a picture" of their depression, and then discuss it with a partner, who would then use the drawing to introduce them to the group as a whole. As expected, the drawings were remarkably diverse, despite the similarity in manifest symptoms among group members, providing eloquent evidence that each related to his or her loss in a highly individualized way.

Josh's hastily drawn picture appears below. To me, his simple felt pen drawing spoke volumes about this ordinarily reticent young man, hinting at the way in which he struggled angrily but ineffectually against the "straight jacket" of his loss. Josh's sense of containment in his suffering and separation from the world were suggested by the almost "electrified" frame around the darkly clad central figure. Moreover, the figure seemed both tormented and sanctified by the "arrows" surrounding his head like the halos in the medieval paintings of martyrs who kept their faith even at the pain of death. Finally, the pierced heart below the figure functioned almost as an explanatory footnote, pointing symbolically toward the lost love that was responsible for Josh's current fate. As the group posed questions and ventured guesses to Josh about the significance of these and other aspects of the drawing, he began to speak of the unique suffering associated with his loss for the first time, and grasp the ways in which it was both similar to and different than the distress of others.

Variations: Any artistic medium can serve as a vehicle for representing loss, drawing on the distinctive talents of the "artist." For example, Carol at first conveyed the keen sense of personal fragmentation resulting from the severed and abusive relationships of her life through a symbolic collage, whose inconsistent and emotionally wrenching images torn from the pages of magazines were attached to the pieces of a broken frame. As her journey toward healing continued, she supplemented this and similar images with jigsaw like compositions whose fragments were gradually woven or spanned with rope or wire, which suggested the growing coherence in her sense of self. Finally, she connected images and words with a series of photographs accompanied by simple but telling poems that captured and conveyed her newfound sense of serenity. Eventually, her compositions took on public as well as private meaning when she donated several of them to an art fair organized by the local mental health association, with proceeds from their sale being used to support needed initiatives for those with no access to psychological services. Carol's example provides a telling illustration of how artistic productions can embody not only a range of deeply personal feelings, but also play a role in consolidating a new and preferred identity as someone who again has something to give to others.

Precautions: Because most persons (especially adults) are unaccustomed to artistic self-expression, it is important to approach such tasks with an attitude of acceptance and curiosity about whatever results. As in creative writing, the product is ultimately less important than the process, as considerable meaning can be condensed into images that have value only for the person producing them. Moreover, care must be taken in the interpretation of artistic productions, with ultimate respect being accorded to the significance placed on them by their creators, rather than by outside observers or commentators, whether lay or professional.

My drawing of my grief:

To me, it symbolizes:

_____
_____
_____
_____
_____
_____
_____

Epitaphs

Indications: In the numbing days and weeks following the death of someone we love, we may be unable to formulate an epitaph that uniquely captures his or her meaning for those left behind. But often an appropriately chosen inscription for a grave marker can focus and affirm the meaning of a relationship, whether or not it ever is actually chiseled in stone. Such epitaphs can be personal creations, or apt discoveries, sometimes encountered when one is not consciously looking for a suitable phrase or expression to memorialize a loss.

Example: Karen had struggled for months to find a suitable epitaph for the gravestone of her severely disabled 8 year old son, Kenny, who died of pneumonia after a long decline. The caretaking Kenny required throughout his life had physically and emotionally exhausted Karen, especially since the accidental death of her husband two years before. Further complicating her mourning was the well intended but hurtful "consolation" offered by others, who noted that she would be "better off" without the burden of caring for him, so that she could give more attention to her remaining "normal" child. As she gradually began to sort out the tangle of feelings that clustered around this loss in the context of our counseling, Karen was surprised to discover in the pages of a book she was casually scanning a pithy sentence that, for her, precisely summarized the place her dead child had held in her life: *Sometimes the richest things can come into our lives from places we would never choose to go.* This then became the inscription she had carved on his headstone, bringing "closure" to a felt obligation she had previously been unable to meet.

Precautions: Because of the high degree of condensation of meaning required by an epitaph, it should be chosen carefully, and in no way hurried in order to bring premature closure to a loss. Trying to formulate the significance of a relationship too succinctly or quickly can overly simplify a complex experience, blinding us to nuances that might be more adequately expressed in somewhat lengthier forms of reflective writing. Sometimes a suitable epitaph will arise spontaneously in the course of poetic self-expression or journalling, or even in reading relevant literature of loss. For this reason, the therapeutic writing of an epitaph might best be reserved for persons who are well along in their grief, and who have had a chance to process it more thoroughly. [5]

Epitaph for: _____

_____

_____

_____

_____

_____

_____

_____

Journals

Indications: Especially when losses are traumatic, they may be difficult to discuss or even disclose to another. And yet the psychological and physical burden of harboring painful memories without the release of sharing can prove far more destructive in the long run. A growing volume of research now supports the conclusion that writing about such traumas as sudden bereavement, personal or parental divorce, interpersonal abandonment or abuse, humiliation and job loss, and even sexual assault can have substantial positive implications for one's emotional and physical health, dramatically increasing one's sense of well-being, and even improving one's immune system functioning. [6] But to enjoy these payoffs, not just any form of writing will do. To benefit from the "write stuff," certain guidelines should be followed, including:

1. *Focus on a loss that is among the more upsetting or traumatic experiences of your entire life.* The more significant the event about which you write, the more beneficial the experience is likely to be.

2. *Write about those aspects of the experience that you have discussed least adequately with others, perhaps aspects that you could never imagine discussing with anyone.* Confessing these suppressed memories is good for more than the soul, even if you confess them in writing only to yourself.

3. *Write from the standpoint of your deepest thoughts and feelings, tacking back and forth between an explicit account of the event and your reactions to it.* Shifting your attention in this way from an external to an internal view may prove more effective than concentrating only on feelings disconnected from experiences, or objective facts divorced from your emotional responses.

4. *Abandon a concern with grammar, spelling, penmanship or typographic accuracy.* What counts is your engagement with the material, not its neatness or literary merit.

5. *Write for at least fifteen minutes per day, for at least four days.* Revisiting the loss seems to promote meaning making in a way that a single telling does not. Allow the content and form of the writing to change, even to shift to other traumatic experiences, across the writing. If a block devel-

ops, write about the block itself, and then try to identify what experience or feeling is behind it.

6. *Schedule a transitional activity after the writing, before resuming "life as usual."* Bear in mind that in the short run, keeping a journal of such traumatic memories is likely to be painful and may even lead to further ruminations about the event, so don't expect yourself to simply get up from the desk, and head to work or begin preparing dinner for the family. Instead, schedule a "buffer period" after the writing, perhaps in the form of a visit with a trusted confidant, a private walk, exercise, or some other activity that doesn't require you to be instantly "put back together" at an emotional level.

Example: Carol was referred to therapy for a severe and unremitting depression that left her unresponsive to either pain or pleasure, to the point that she felt the need to cut or burn herself in order to feel alive. She felt radically estranged and distrustful of others, and increasingly preoccupied with an internal drama consisting of tortured recollections of childhood traumas and recent abuse by a man she loved. And yet it seemed impossible for her initially to share these painful secrets, even in the confidential context of psychotherapy. With my gentle prompting, however, she began to divulge them in a personal journal, which she gradually began to share with me.

Writing daily, Carol at first vividly expressed her self-loathing associated with the painful events of her past, eventually distilling an account of her incest experiences, the death of her father, her psychological abuse by the religious cult that lured her in adolescence, and the degrading sexual relationship with a man that ensued. At first, the writing was associated with acute anguish, visible in the pressured and uneven hand in which she wrote. But across time, the writing took on a more reflective and even lyrical quality, as she chronicled her long climb toward self-respect and the reconstruction of her relational life. Carol's journal reflected this gradual overall shift toward accommodation of her losses and integration of her life, but also recorded the occasional setbacks she encountered on her journey toward self-affirmation.

While Carol's story is a dramatic one, the use of journals can be extended quite easily to more normative life stories, and narratives that revolve around less profound, but nonetheless important losses. For example, Andrew, a 47 year old administrator within a health care system, lost his job when his department "reorganized." Even with a stable history of personal and family adjustment, he found the resulting shift to self-employment bruising, and felt consumed by anger and resentment over the job loss itself, as well as the inevitable hurdles to successful self-employment. For him, a week's worth of daily journal entries helped him vent his sense of betrayal by his employer and anxiety about the future that he felt the need to control at other times. Moreover, he discovered that the writing gradually changed form over time, moving from an expressive, cathartic style to a greater emphasis on problem-solving. As often happens, this private journal work led to spontaneous conversations with his wife about their finances, and a mutual plan to work together to weather a difficult period of adjustment as a family.

Variations: While the highly expressive and personal exploration of loss in daily journal entries is encouraged above, there are many other forms of diary work that can help one sort out the lessons of loss. For instance, passionate self disclosure can alternate with more calculated and planful brainstorming, as in Andrew's case, or one can use such writing to sift through the significant emotional events of the day or week, sometimes discovering their hidden connections to previous loss experiences. Alternatively, you can keep a dream journal that captures and interprets significant dreams (e.g., pursing the fleeting image of a deceased father in the attic of one's childhood home). [7] Several other forms of expressive writing described in this chapter can be used to prime or integrate the kind of journal entries emphasized in this application, so that you should feel free to draw upon various forms according to your purposes. In some cases, any form of writing may seem too constraining, so that variations involving tape recording one's entries might be worth considering.

Precautions: In addition to the caveats outlined above (e.g., the usefulness of scheduling buffer activities following intensive writing), it is often helpful to secure the privacy of your journal, so that you can feel truly free to write in an uninhibited fashion. Remember that the primary audience for your writing is yourself, so that it need not ever be shared with another to have a long-term benefit for you. Some persons even find it reassuring to destroy their "confessions" after committing them to paper, although this has the drawback of eliminating a possible source of future reflection and a tangible record of personal growth.

A second precaution concerns the goodness of fit of this, or any, personal application for the individual user. Because intensive emotional writing can leave you temporarily feeling "raw" and vulnerable, even if it promotes long-term adjustment, it is probably best to postpone such writing until you feel relatively "together," rather than in the immediate aftermath of a major loss. As a corollary of this, counselors working with clients who are markedly unstable are encouraged to use such writing advisedly; I introduced this dimension of our work to Carol only after we had begun to establish a secure and ongoing therapeutic relationship. Even when I use such writing as a part of therapy, I continue to respect my clients' right to privacy concerning whether or not to share any particular entry with me in the course of our sessions.

Life Imprint

Indications: Although people in western cultures are accustomed to thinking of themselves as "individuals," proud of their distinctiveness from others, in fact we all represent "pastiche personalities," reflecting characteristics modeled on an enormous range of persons who have been important to us. Without really intending it, from our first days of life we appropriate ways of gesturing, thinking, speaking, feeling, and acting from our parents, relatives, friends, and even public figures with whom we identify. In a sense, then, we become living memorials to these persons, even after they themselves have died. Noting the imprint that such people have made on our own lives can be a powerful way of honoring their contribution, forming a living web of connection that we, through our lives, extend to others. [8]

Variations: While we naturally can recognize in ourselves many of the mannerisms, tastes, and values of our parents, the imprint that one life makes on another is by no means simply one of inheritance in a genetic sense. For example, the reverse pattern of "inheriting" a sense of love, loyalty, or the preciousness of life from their children is often reported by bereaved parents, and important mentors or teachers can often be a source of identification even when they are unrelated to us in any biological sense. Thus, tracing the impact of a friend's life on our own can be as legitimate as examining the imprint of our parents, although the former contribution to our sense of self may be more abstract than the latter.

Precautions: Not all imprints are positive, precisely because some relationships may be troubled or ambivalent. As a result, we may sometimes trace our sense of self-doubt, our drivenness, our sarcastic tone of voice, or our proneness to anger to the model provided by a critical parent, or find the origin of our distrust of others in the opinions held by an influential friend. But even in such cases it is often helpful to recognize that these negative imprints arose outside us, and perhaps can be resisted and transformed through personal effort. In addition, even these negative instances are typically accompanied by compensatory strengths modeled on these same figures, which we can selectively affirm and retain. However, sorting out the mixed imprint of ambivalent relationships can be a difficult task, one that sometimes requires the assistance of a professional counselor.

The person whose imprint I want to trace is: _____

This person has had the following impact on:

my mannerisms and gestures:

_____
_____
_____
_____
_____

my way of speaking and communicating:

_____
_____
_____
_____
_____

my work and pastime activities:

_____
_____
_____
_____
_____

my basic personality:

_____
_____
_____
_____
_____

my values and beliefs:

_____
_____
_____
_____
_____
_____

The imprints I would most like to affirm and maintain are:

_____
_____
_____
_____
_____
_____

The imprints I would most like to relinquish or change are:

_____
_____
_____
_____
_____

Linking Objects

Indications: We are often comforted by preserving in our lives objects that belonged to the persons we have lost, and quite naturally tend to accumulate keepsakes and mementos of people and times that have gone before. Occasionally it is helpful to adopt this as a conscious strategy for responding to loss, by making deliberate decisions about how to integrate cherished "linking objects" into our ongoing lives.

Example: When Karen's son Kenny died after an eight-year course of disability and illness, she was unable to contemplate "cleaning out his room" for some months afterward. But as she came to feel more resolved about the meaning of his life and death over the course of grief counseling, she began to feel that doing so represented a logical next step in her healing. With minimal prompting by me, Karen solicited the help of her teenage daughter to sort through Kenny's belongings, choosing those that would be offered to specific family members and friends, and others that would be donated to charity. However, Karen wisely decided to keep several toys of special significance, such as stuffed animals that had comforted her young son during his protracted hospitalizations, placing them in a simple glass display case in the room that she then converted into a study. The decision to use Kenny's toys both to continue her emotional bond with her child and to extend the same symbolic ties to other members of the family allowed Karen to find an appropriate place for Kenny in her changed life, in a way that she felt he would approve. Making such decisions in discussion with her daughter also facilitated shared reminiscences, tears, laughter, and hugs that helped the two remaining family members come together in their grief, and reflect jointly on Kenny's place in their broader family system.

Variations: Not all ways of linking to the memory of lost loved ones needs to be through objects, per se. Natalie Cole's moving posthumous duet with the voice of her father, Nat King Cole, is truly an "unforgettable" example of the harmonious blending of the voices of generations. Likewise, Martin Luther King III's decision to carry on his father's civil rights advocacy maintains his sense of connection to his father's mission through an extension of his life's work. Thus, linkages may be expressed in forms as concrete as wearing a favorite piece of jewelry or clothing of a deceased parent, or as abstract as following through on his or her vision or life projects.

Precautions: While deeply meaningful, the cultivation of connection with one who has died can become problematic if taken to the extreme. [9] This is particularly the case when the attempt to incorporate the concerns of the lost loved one leads to a neglect of one's own, or when identification is taken to such an extent that one becomes morbidly preoccupied with our personal susceptibility to the disease that took our loved one's life. Similarly, an inability to let go of any of the possessions of a loved one may suggest a failure to acknowledge necessary changes in oneself and one's life in the wake of loss, as if one's identity were frozen from that point forward. In such cases it is usually more enlightened to try to understand the meaning of the continued connection and promote more discriminating and symbolic forms of bonding, than it is to try to force a "letting go" on the part of the reluctant mourner.

I can maintain a linkage to the person or life I have lost by:

_____

_____

_____

_____

_____

_____

I can allow myself to change by:

_____

_____

_____

_____

_____

_____

Loss Characterizations

Indications: As an in-depth narrative technique for exploring loss and its impact on personal identity, the Loss Characterization can be used as an adjunct to grief therapy, or as a guided process of self-discovery. In a counseling context, it is indicated whenever we want to understand the bereaved person's adaptation to loss in his or her own terms, with minimum imposition of structure by the counselor. The Loss Characterization consists simply of an open-ended instructional prompt, presented at the top of an otherwise blank sheet of paper. The respondent is then given maximum leeway to respond as he or she sees fit, producing a narrative account that can be interrogated for meaning in more or less formal ways. The instructional set is as follows:

> In the space that follows, please write a character sketch of _____ [your name], in light of her loss. Write it just as if she were the principal character in a book, movie, or play. Write it as it might be written by a friend who knew her very intimately and very sympathetically, perhaps better than anyone really could know her. Be sure to write it in the third person. For example, start out by saying "_____ is..."

The wording of these instructions is chosen carefully to invite discussion of some of the major themes running through the person's construction of life and self. [10] Thus, the term "character sketch" is intended to suggest a narrative that is pertinent to the respondent's sense of who she is, but also to imply that the sketch need not be a definitive or encyclopedic autobiography. The invitation to describe the main character "in light of her loss" focuses attention on the relevance of the bereavement experience, but without implying any particular relationship to the loss as negative or positive. Likewise, the open-endedness of the exercise permits the writer to focus on any aspect of her experience, rather than "pulling" for any particular set of reactions of presumed importance. In adopting the imaginary viewpoint of a sympathetic and intimate friend, the author is encouraged to disclose relatively deep-going observations about herself and her life, but to suspend a posture of self-criticism or condemnation. Finally, by adopting a third rather than first person perspective, the Loss Characterization prompts the respondent to take perspective on her life, providing a broader context than might be yielded by a first person account. Overall, it is assumed that the instructional set invites a person to work on the "growing edges" of her system, focusing on those constructions of self and life that have enough uncertainty to make exploration interesting, but enough structure to make it meaningful. The resulting sketch can then be used as a starting point for a personal loss journal, as a way of identifying themes worthy of attention in grief counseling, or as a source of "data" for more elaborate qualitative analysis, as illustrated below.

Example: The Loss Characterization of Kerry is presented below, along with some interpretive commentary. Kerry completed the exercise approximately three years after the death of her son, Jacob, whose congenital heart failure finally caused his death at age two.

Kerry is a woman who feels and experiences her life deeply inside herself. Prior to the loss of her son, Kerry led what appeared to be a "charmed" life. From all outside appearances, everything in her life was easy and beautiful. Inside, however, deep inside, she knew that something was inferior about her life and the manner in which she was living it. Even though the external rewards of financial security and social belongingness (and the coinciding pressures to maintain them) were abundant in her existence, she still didn't feel at one with herself or with others. There was always that little part of her that felt something was wrong. She was doing something wrong. She could see others who appeared to have a depth and intelligence about themselves that she was somehow lacking and there was a negative moral attachment to that. Something about her was wrong and inferior and she knew it. But she couldn't get to it.

In high school, the mother of Kerry's best friend died. Like many of Kerry's other friends, Cathy was popular and well liked by others, but always troubled by her own life. For Kerry this was a puzzling juxtaposition in life: people with trouble and tragedy in their lives who weren't very happy were very loved by others. Those like herself, however, who were living what appeared to be quintessentially "normal" (often boring) lives, did not have the depth of feeling and magnetism of experience these other people seemed to embody. For years she naively wished that she too could have that special something in her life. (She didn't realize what a price the others had paid). Finally, at age 34 her wish came true. She had the chance to experience and develop that depth and inner intelligence that she had seen for so long in others. Her second child, Jacob, was born.

Throughout his life, Kerry lived in a mode of survival. But she didn't know it. It was just life to her and after a while, it seemed altogether normal. On some level, retrospectively, Kerry had to give up her own life for those years in order for Jacob to live and for the experience to ripen into vintage possibility for her soul's education.

For 23 months Kerry lived a life where at any moment she might have to (and did many times) jump into her car and head for the emergency room because Jacob was looking a little blue, literally. She always prayed on the way to the hospital that this time they could just examine Jacob, change his medicines or something and send them back home, but no visit ever lasted for less than two weeks. Some nights lying on the fold out bed in Jacob's hospital room for the twelfth night in a row, she would cry over how unfair this all was and how badly she wanted to go home and sleep in her own bed and be taken care of herself. But she had no choice in the matter. No choice!!! She had no choice but to stay with her son who needed her so desperately, as she was the only one who was so finely tuned into him that she could see trouble coming for him and help prevent the problem. Many times she wanted to leave, to escape, but she knew for the first time in her life that there was something she couldn't do, a choice she wasn't free to make. She was stuck in her very intense and exhausting and sometimes frightening life.

Usually, during these hospital stays, Kerry would stay full time, except in the evening when her husband would come and relieve her for a few hours. She would go home and see her darling Sarah who had long since given up wondering where Mommy had gone and when she'd be back. Oh God, she would scream and thrash inside at her inability to take this pain away from her daughter. She would give anything if she could make Sarah's life free of pain. But she couldn't do it. Learning what pain was about was a new lesson for Kerry and a difficult one for her to see happening in the young life of her three year old daughter. Usually, Kerry would anesthetize herself with a little wine while she was home with Sarah, and then when Sarah was in bed, it was coffee, wake back up, because she was back on duty!! Usually for the entire night. When did she sleep? I don't know, but it wasn't very often or ever for very long. During these entire 23 months, Kerry and her family had love and support from many people they knew and even from some they didn't know. And when Jacob died, the same was true for the most part, although there were those who couldn't tolerate the painful knowledge this brought.

Once the death occurred, Kerry began to desperately search for reasons why this happened to her (and her family). Twenty-nine years before, when her own mother was twenty-nine years old, Kerry lost a sibling who died just after birth. Kerry was almost exactly the same age as Sarah when they each lost siblings. As Kerry began to reexamine and reevaluate her own "normal" life in light of this loss, she could not ignore the synchronicity of events that was becoming apparent to her. She began to envision God as a "great karmic cashier in the sky". He (and make no mistake, it was "He" at that time) would say to her "There's a debt due here and someone is going to pay. You can pay me now or you can pay me later, but someone is going to pay. And there's interest due!!" Kerry began to recognize that despite her lifelong success at hiding the pain in her interior life, even from herself, it was time to "ante-up." She knew that if she did not pay for the sin of unconsciousness bequeathed to her by her mother and her mother's mother that sweet, darling, innocent Sarah would be forced to pay the debt of the feminine unconsciousness in this matrilineal line. As much as Kerry did eventually learn the positive value of knowing pain, she did not want to pass this one on to her daughter. She became determined to live her life and parent her children as consciously as she possibly could.

There was a great price of suffering to pay for the consciousness which Kerry now possesses. She paid it in the loss of Jacob, in the loss of friends who couldn't stand the pain, in the loss of a way of life in which she had previously been fairly comfortable. And despite her attempts to be a loving wife and friend, at times even those closest around her do not understand the rage she has felt these last years, nor the changes that have occurred in the interior alchemical fire of her soul.

In a very real sense, a Loss Characterization like Kerry's speaks for itself: it provides an immediately accessible portrayal of the author's bereavement experience, with an emphasis on how it both shaped and was shaped by his or her personal identity. When used in a counseling context, the exercise provides a point of entry into a delicate tapestry of meaning woven around the loss, inviting further therapeutic questions that help unfold the experience of bereavement in greater detail.

But as helpful as this informal use of the Loss Characterization can be as a "homework assignment" in grief counseling, it is often revealing to subject the narrative to more formal qualitative analysis. In the case of the present illustration, I will use several *guideline questions* as prompts to examine Kerry's construing of her loss experience in greater detail, recognizing that these represent only a subset of a larger set of questions that might be asked in analyzing her characterization. Because this more detailed kind of analysis is likely to take place in a grief therapy setting, I will discuss its implications for Kerry as a client, although many of the same questions can serve as useful prompts for self-exploration when the exercise is used as a form of self-help, as described below.

   1. Start with a credulous approach, asking, "What does the world look like through Kerry's eyes?" If we suspend a preoccupation with whether Kerry's adaptation to her son's death is healthy or unhealthy, normal or complicated, we are freed to empathically explore her unique vision of the world and her place in it. From her characterization, Kerry's world would appear to be a somewhat lonely place, a place of private struggle, though a struggle rich in meaning. It is a world filled with cosmological significance, in which important life events are purposeful and nonrandom, even when they bring pain.

   2. Observe the sequence and transition, interpreting the protocol as a flowing whole, with apparent breaks considered as unexpected elaborations of the major theme(s). Rather than giving a straightforward chronological account, Kerry places her loss experience in the first paragraph against the backdrop of a problem to be solved, namely, her sense that "something was wrong" with her life, despite its external "abundance." She then elaborates on this in the second paragraph with her long-standing observation that "people with trouble and tragedy in their lives [are] very loved by others." Jacob's birth, life, and death are then introduced as a kind of personal resolution of this paradox in the main body of the Loss Characterization, before she concludes by reflecting on the spiritual and cosmological implications of this life-changing event in the closing paragraphs. Thus, even the form of her writing suggests an attempt to frame the experience in a way that gives it meaning and relative "closure."

   3. Look for repeated terms with similar content, which may point toward an important theme that is not fully articulated. Kerry's protocol is filled with references to "intense," "painful," "frightening," and "desperate" feelings, as well as allusions to her "crying," "thrashing," and displaying "rage" in response to her situation. While the salience of these turbulent emotional experiences is muted somewhat by the narrative flow of her account, the recurrent presence of these terms suggests the importance of this "alchemical fire" in fostering her wished-for self-transformation. By implication, the counselor is encouraged to consider painful affect a potentially constructive experience for Kerry, rather than a problem to be controlled or eliminated. However, there is a conspicuous absence of references to others understanding (or even witnessing) these feelings, and at least one explicit statement that they do not. This suggests that the whole question of the social validation for her inner life may be a worthwhile topic for therapeutic discussion.

4. Shift the emphasis on different parts of key sentences, as a prompt to consider different "readings" of their meaning. This guideline can help broaden the interpretive focus of the analysis, which might be unintentionally constricted by a single reading. To take but one example, consider the differing nuances of Kerry's opening sentence if read with the following two emphases: (a) Kerry is a woman who *feels* and experiences her life deeply inside herself. (b) Kerry is a woman who feels and experiences her life deeply *inside* herself. While the first underscores the critical role of emotionality noted above, the second points up the interiority of her life, and perhaps the struggle to share it with others. This latter implication is considered in greater detail below.

5. What are the primary dimensions of meaning implied in the protocol, and what essential tensions does this suggest in the client's life and loss experience? If we assume that our meaning systems are organized in terms of personally significant contrasts that thematize significant life events, then what sorts of constructs does the author apply to construe her self and circumstances? Kerry's protocol contains a rich network of such constructs, including contrasts between "inside vs. outside" views of her life, an apparently "charmed vs. inferior" existence, a distinction between "troubled vs. normal" persons, as well as between those who are "loved vs. have no magnetism." A recurrent contrast between "depth and inner intelligence" on the one hand, and "unconsciousness" on the other seems to subsume several of these dimensions, implying a distinction between ways of living that are superficially charmed and normal, but ultimately unconscious and unloved, and a more troubled and painful mode of existence, but one that permits more inward depth, as well as more loving relationships with others. Kerry views herself as having used her loss to move from the former constellation to the latter.

6. How is the author's meaning system challenged or supported by the loss, and who emerges as important validating agents for her current self-understandings? In Kerry's case, Jacob's birth and death powerfully undercut the superficial "normality" of her life, although at a deeper level, her caretaking toward him was coherent with her profound wish for greater self-awareness. While reference is made to the "love and support" the family received from "those they knew as well as those they didn't know," the lack of mention of more than temporary support from *within* the family may be noteworthy. Nor is it clear who inside or outside the family affirms the meaning she has made of her son's death, or her attempted reconstruction of her identity in light of the loss.

7. Examine the author's explanatory style, particularly his or her attributions for the loss itself. For Kerry, as for most bereaved persons, the quest for a satisfying answer to the question of why her loved one died is a central theme of both her life and her account of it in the Loss Characterization. While Kerry experienced Jacob's illness and death and her own immersion in caretaking as clearly unchosen, she nonetheless sought a psychospiritual framework within which to give this compelling chapter of her life a broader meaning. She found such a framework in a personal cosmology centering around a stern male God who exacted a steep karmic price for the depth and inner intelligence she had fervently sought—a price that entailed the loss of a once "comfortable" life, a social circle of friends, and her beloved son. However, these sacrifices were ultimately balanced by both direct and indirect compensations, in terms of mitigating the suffering of her son (and daughter), and more abstractly (but equally powerfully), breaking a transgenerational cycle of matrilineal "unconsciousness," permitting both her and her daughter to live with greater genuineness and self-awareness than had her mother before her (at least from the point of her mother's own bereavement onward). From a constructivist standpoint, the "validity" of this construction is not at issue, and is in any case incontestable. What is relevant is that Kerry found validation for this explanation in the meaningful coincidences of the circumstances surrounding the deaths of her son and her sister twenty-nine years earlier, and that this account rendered her loss coherent with her biography, which both preceded and followed her son's short life. Having given up so much in her life, she was able ultimately to harvest the lessons of her loss, and allow "the experience to ripen into vintage possibility for her soul's education."

Variations: The Loss Characterization can easily be integrated into grief therapy, where it can bring to light a number of themes or issues of relevance for further therapeutic processing. However, it can also be used as a way to begin or deepen a personal journal to explore the implications of loss for one's changed sense of self, whether or not one follows up with the "guideline questions" to interrogate its meaning in detail.

While the above illustration focuses on a major loss through death, the technique can easily be adapted to other forms of loss by simply varying the instructions slightly to refer to a self characterization written in light of one's divorce, job loss, or relocation. Finally, the repetition of the exercise at various intervals after the loss (e.g., on successive anniversaries) can provide a way of tracing and affirming progress in "relearning the self" over time.

Precautions: Persons using the Loss Characterization should resist the temptation to focus only on their weaknesses or vulnerabilities, although these can be acknowledged alongside their strengths. Overall, the technique is designed to be descriptive rather than evaluative, and to begin to help the person configure an account of the unwanted transition brought about by the loss, and thereby to begin to give it meaning. Uses of the sketch to identify the author's "distorted thinking" or "neurotic tendencies" are therefore inappropriate and should be avoided.

Your Loss Characterization

In the space that follows, please write a character sketch of
_____ [your name], in light of his or her loss. Write it just as
if he or she were the principal character in a book, movie, or play. Write it
as it might be written by a friend who knew him or her very intimately and
very sympathetically, perhaps better than anyone really could. Be sure to
write it in the third person. For example, start out by saying
"_____ is..."

_____
_____
_____
_____
_____
_____
_____
_____
_____
_____
_____
_____
_____
_____
_____
_____
_____
_____
_____
_____
_____
_____
_____
_____
_____
_____
_____

Guideline Questions

1. What does the world look like through the eyes of this character?

_____

_____

_____

_____

_____

_____

_____

_____

2. Are there any unexpected breaks in the story? Are there any themes or issues that could in some way bridge them?

_____

_____

_____

_____

_____

_____

_____

3. Are there any similar terms that are used repeatedly in the account, which might point to an important underlying issue?

_____

_____

_____

_____

_____

_____

4. Shift the emphasis on different words or phrases in key sentences. Does this suggest any alternative readings of this material?

_____

_____

_____

_____

_____

_____

_____

_____

_____

_____

_____

5. What are the major contrasts or dimensions implied in this sketch? What does this suggest about the character's perceived alternatives?

_____

_____

_____

_____

_____

_____

_____

_____

_____

_____

_____

6. In what ways did the loss challenge the character's assumptive world, or sense of self? Who supports the character's way of accommodating to the loss, and how?

_____

_____

_____

_____

_____

_____

_____

_____

_____

_____

_____

7. How does the character answer the question of why the loss occurred? Has this explanation changed over time?

_____

_____

_____

_____

_____

_____

_____

_____

_____

_____

_____

Meaning Reconstruction "Interview"

Indications: The questions that follow provide a general interview structure for beginning a course of grief counseling along meaning reconstruction lines. I have tried to suggest some representative inquiries under three headings: *Entry* questions (to help you move into the experiential world of the client's grieving), *explanation* questions (to extend these preliminary inquiries into a greater concern with meaning making), and *elaboration* questions to promote broader perspective taking regarding the loss). Some persons find the process of formulating responses to these questions to be therapeutically powerful in itself, over and above its value as an "assessment" for the sake of the counselor.

Variations: Bereaved persons may find these questions helpful prompts for their own reflective writing about their loss, even if no counselor is involved in the process. In addition, some of these questions might be assigned as a between-session assignment in grief counseling, rather than being used as an interview structure, per se.

Precautions: I have found it most helpful to use two or three of the questions under each category to prompt my initial inquiries into a client's experience, selecting those that seem most appropriate to his or her case. However, I typically use these only as points of departure into our conversation, and urge both bereaved persons and grief counselors not to feel "straight jacketed" by the need to "stick with the structure" when diverging from it would seem more appropriate.

Entry Questions

- What experience of death or loss would you like to explore?

_____

_____

_____

_____

- What do you recall about how you responded to the event at the time?

_____

_____

_____

_____

- How did your feelings about it change over time?

_____

_____

_____

_____

- How did others in your life at that time respond to the loss? To your reactions to it?

_____

_____

_____

_____

- Who *were* you at the time of the loss, at the level of your basic personality, stage of development, and central concerns?

_____

_____

_____

_____

- What was the most painful part of the experience to you?

_____

_____

_____

Explanation Questions

• How did you make sense of the death or loss at the time?

_____

_____

_____

_____

• How do you interpret the loss now?

_____

_____

_____

• What philosophical or spiritual beliefs contributed to your adjustment to this loss? How were they affected by it, in turn?

_____

_____

_____

_____

Elaboration questions

• How has this experience affected your sense of priorities?

_____

_____

_____

_____

• How has this experience affected your view of yourself or your world?

_____

_____

_____

_____

- What lessons about loving has this person or this loss taught you?

_____

_____

_____

_____

- How would your life be different if this person had lived/this loss did not occur?

_____

_____

_____

_____

- Are there any steps that you could take that would be helpful or healing now?

_____

_____

_____

_____

_____

_____

_____

_____

Memory Books

Indications: One means of honoring a lost loved one is to construct a "memory book" capturing one's thoughts, feelings, and recollections about him or her, perhaps in the form of a scrapbook that may also contain mementos or photographs of his or her life. Unlike more open ended journals and forms of expressive writing that focus more on the author's private experience, memory books typically represent memorials that can be more easily shared with or even compiled by multiple persons. In a sense, they represent an extension of a birth or wedding album, but with a focus on the last of life's transitions, rather than one of the first. While memory books can be compiled according to the personal preferences of their authors, it is sometimes useful to begin with basic background information about the one who has died, such as name, date of birth, place of birth, and family members. Later pages can be titled with prompts for a certain kind of recollection or reflection. For example, prompts might include such statements as:

- My first memory of you was...
- My favorite times with you were...
- What I love most about you is...
- What others say about you is...
- Your favorite activities were...
- Your favorite words of wisdom were...
- When I think of you, I...
- I keep your memory alive by...

A useful memory book should also have plenty of blank pages, permitting free form entries according to the author's purpose. [11]

Variations: In more therapeutic applications, this basic scheme can be expanded to encourage processing of ambivalent aspects of the relationship, using prompts like:

- What I most regret about our relationship is...
- What I never heard you say was...
- What I wish you could hear is...

- You most disappointed me when...
- My most troubling memory of you was when...
- I know that I am moving ahead when...

Memory books can be compiled by whole families, by asking other family members to contribute a page or chapter to the book, and can be expanded to include artwork or photographs at the author's discretion. Audio "books" can also be compiled in a similar structure using tape recorded reflections in cases where writing is infeasible, or when capturing the sound of someone's voice adds a special dimension to the project.

Precautions: Because they are often shared with others, memory books can be constraining, especially when the "whole story" of the relationship is a difficult one to tell or hear. Even in the best of relationships, there are typically a few "rough edges," and it can be hard to accommodate these in an album of "cherished memories." Thus, constructing such a volume of re-membrance should be reserved for substantially positive relationships, or at least be supplemented by separate therapeutic writing that is kept in a less public forum.

Metaphoric Images

Indications: Sometimes literal words fail us in conveying our unique sense of loss—we may feel depressed, desolate, alone, or angry, but the character of our own grief is somehow more than just the sum of these standard descriptions. To move beyond the constraints of public speech, we need to use words in a more personal way, and draw on terms that are rich in resonance and imagery. Speaking of our loss metaphorically can help us accomplish this, sometimes leading to surprising insights unavailable to us when we think of it only in more conventional, "symptomatic" terms.

Example: For most of her childhood and adolescence, Sara's grandfather had been a source of humor, inspiration and strength to her, a touchstone of balance in a world that was sometimes emotionally confusing and chaotic. When her grandfather died, Sara felt the loss keenly, but integrated it as part of her rich family history, and moved forward into an adult identity of which her grandfather undoubtedly would have been proud. Still, many years later, she recognized that the legacy of this loss was with her still, and formulated the following metaphor to convey how she currently carried her grief.

Sara's Suitcase

My grief is like an old-fashioned hard-sided suitcase. It's lined with silky faded burgundy material and little elastic pockets attached to the sides for storing small trinkets or precious items you would want to keep safe during your travels. For me, that captures the way we can carry our grief around with us. Even when we think we have unpacked it completely, we can still find something surprising hidden away in one of those side compartments, maybe something we haven't seen or thought about for years.

One of the great advantages of metaphor is that it can compress a great deal of meaning into an economical expression or image, which can in turn be expanded by focusing on its elements and implications. Thus, it could prove valuable to explore with Sara whether her style of accommodating to loss was "old-fashioned" in other ways, whether the suitcase used in the metaphor might actually resemble one used by her grandfather, thereby linking her symbolically to his memory, what sorts of things might be found in the side pockets of the suitcase, what things might have been "misplaced" at the time of the loss that might yet be discovered, and so on. As in the other exercises described in this chapter, metaphors of loss should be taken as bridges into the bereaved person's world of meaning, with the counselor serving as a respectful fellow traveler, rather than authoritative guide to their significance.

Variations: It can also be valuable to use loss metaphors in support groups for bereaved persons, where they can serve as surprisingly intimate icebreakers for further discussion If used as part of a group "round," with the group facilitator briefly asking "curious questions" about the image, they can also function as metaphoric means of deepening members' understanding of one another's unique experience of loss. The following illustration was excerpted from a few minutes of discussion in one such group.

Kenya's Rock

Counselor: Kenya, how would you describe your grief, if you tried to picture it as some form of image or object? What would it look like?

Kenya: For me, it's just like some enormous weight, like a big stone or rock of some kind.

Counselor: Hmm. And where are you in relation to this rock, in your image?

Kenya: Well, I guess I'm sort of underneath it, like it's on top of me.

Counselor: And can you feel its weight? How do you see yourself in the image?

Kenya: It's strange, but it doesn't really feel heavy... [pause]. It's like it's sort of hollowed out on the bottom, you know, and I'm hunkered down in that hollow space. It's not really a bad feeling at all.

Counselor: How does it feel?

Kenya: Kind of, well, protected. Yeah, like it's a big shell or something, keeping out the world, and just letting me be there by myself.

Counselor: That's fascinating.... How do you see other people being positioned in relation to that image?

Kenya: They're all on the outside, my husband, my mother, and lots of other folks, and they're telling me to push the stone off, and some of them are prying or lifting at it. But I don't really want it to move. It's like it's taking care of me.

Counselor: [Looking around the group.] How do the rest of you feel about Kenya's image? Does any part of it surprise you? Do you have any questions for her about it?

Greg (another member): Yeah, I guess I was really surprised by that. I thought her grief would be crushing her, like mine is crushing me, but she seems to almost want to keep it there. What I'd like to know is whether she thinks it's a permanent part of her, or if she'll come out from under it at some point in the future.... [a spirited discussion ensues].

As indicated in this brief excerpt, a few curious follow-up questions can prime further exploration of the implications of any particular image, both on the part of the author of the metaphor, and on the part of those with whom it is being shared.

Precautions: In addition to the general caveat that it is the individual's interpretations of the metaphor that matter, not someone else's, further precautions in the use of loss imagery arise from the nature of metaphor itself. Unlike literal language, which tends to fix meanings and give them stable referents (if I am "bereaved" this week, I must surely be next week as well), figurative language is far more fluid and protean, changing in its nuances in the very act of speaking. For this reason, it is often helpful to ask if there is any form of *movement or change within the image,* and if so, in what direction. For example, Maria described her grief as a kind of constriction around her chest and throat, which she experienced as a physical tightness in her body. When prompted to convey this sense in figurative terms, and to identify any movement associated with the image, she described it as an invisible boa constrictor, gradually suffocating her. This then led us to augment our discussion of the image with active practice in deep breathing, coupled with the self-instruction, "loosen up." Maria found this immensely helpful, and was then able to explore other subtle aspects of the loss experience without feeling suffocated in the process.

My Metaphor for Loss

_____
_____
_____
_____
_____
_____

Is there some way that I experience this image in my body? Where am *I* in the picture? What am I doing, thinking, and feeling?

_____
_____
_____
_____
_____
_____

Where are *other people* in the picture? If they were to enter it, what would they be doing, thinking, and feeling?

_____
_____
_____
_____
_____
_____

Is there any *movement* or direction of change in the image? If continued, where would it lead? Do I have any influence on this direction? Do I want any?

_____
_____
_____
_____
_____
_____

Metaphoric Stories

Indications: Sometimes a single metaphor of loss is so rich that it can be expanded into a short parable or metaphoric story, which captures not only a momentary image of ones' grief, but gives an account of it over time as well. Speaking figuratively, metaphors like those illustrated above give a symbolic *snapshot* of one's grief experience, whereas metaphoric stories represent *movies or documentaries* of one's loss, in a way that gives it a clearer past, present, and future. Such stories can evolve from an image, integrating many of the components teased out above through the use of curious questioning and follow-up prompts.

Example: Steve Ryan is a bereaved father, whose son Sean was born with serious kidney damage in March 1994. [12] Through a life that was desperately difficult for the whole family Sean's good humor and joy in life never deserted him. Steve credits Sean with teaching other family members, by his example, how to live through adversity rather than merely survive. Steve, his wife, Carol, and Sean's older brother, Colin (now six), followed Sean's lead, and the immense pride they came to feel in their family arose from his strength of character. Sean died May 1, 1996 from complications following a kidney transplant. Following his death Steve struggled with the inconsistency between his own feelings and the example Sean set in living his life. He wrote the following metaphoric story, "Three Sided Houses," as a "message to himself" to come to grips with why he should embrace his ongoing life rather than remain immersed in bitter anger and longing for his son's return. His unedited story, printed here with his permission, follows.

Three Sided Houses

I am building a three sided house.
It is not a good design. With one side open to the weather, it will never offer complete shelter from life's cold winds. Four sides would be much better, but there is no foundation on one side, and so three walls are all I have to work with.

I am building this place from the rubble of the house I used to own. It was a warm and solid place and was where I most wanted to be in the world. It had four good walls and would, I thought, withstand the most violent storm.

It did not. A storm beyond my understanding tore my house apart and left the fragments lying on the ground around me.

For some time now I have wandered among the remnants of my life, searching for small reminders of how fine this place used to be. But these ruins do not portray the house that once stood here. No more than gravel in a river can describe the grandeur of the mountain from which the rock was scoured. These shattered pieces say nothing of the warmth that this site used to know.

And yet, it seems a sacrilege to think of building again. Is there not some law of reverence that dictates this land remain barren? No new structure can approach the beauty of the old one. Since that storm tore my house down I have held these broken sticks and stones about me, a shrine to the loss I have endured, excusing any need for me to meet the lesser storms that still must blow across my path.

But it seems to be the way with shrines, the monument itself impairs our vision of the soul we want to touch. We build to mark events and lose our picture of how a life gave consequence to those events. So it is with my own sad memorial. I gather in the wreckage now as if to say that death is the defining moment of my child's existence. In this wretched state I will not forget that he died. But what of remembering how he lived? How hard it is to grasp the beauty of his life from this vantage point of misery. This shabby mound might reflect the condition of my heart, but is does no justice to the memory of my son.

And so I must rebuild. Not, as so many onlookers would suggest, because I need shelter once again. The storm now travels within me, and there is no shelter from that tempest behind doors or walls.

Who can show me how to build here now? There are no architects, no experts in designing three sided houses. Why is it then so many people seem to have advice for me? "Move on," they say, quite convinced that another house can replace the one I lost. Do they not know how completely we are tied to the houses we build? No soul takes kindly to a change in residence and if I "move on" that part of me will stay behind.

I grow weary of consultations based on murky insight, delivered with such confidence. I am told that time heals all, as if this rubble will reassemble by itself if I just bide my time. Some people will approach but stop and point and tell me I must add another wall. As if I had a choice.

I know my neighbors wish more than anything to see me safely housed again. But in truth, they are also troubled by the air of dereliction that this ruin brings down upon the street. If I would just rebuild then they would not be confronted with reminders of nature's cruelty standing in plain view. With each new course of blocks, a quiet sigh of relief. Pressed to disguise the outward evidence of my troubles, I put up siding and install shutters before the framework is in place. Is this outside-in construction the most sensible way for me to build my house? I doubt it.

Among those who wish to see my house rise again there are real heroes too. People who are not daunted by the wreckage. It is not a pleasant role for them to play because the dust clings to those who come to see me and it will not wash off when they go home. They understand that fourth wall is gone forever, and they make no pretense otherwise. They are willing to remember with me how fine this house used to be. And they will help me with the boulders as I struggle to nudge them back into place. Above all they know how difficult this task is and no suggestion comes from them about how far along I ought to be.

As I look out at the job that lies before me, the will to carry out this project is slow to come. I toiled to build my first house and yet I know that this one will be so much harder to erect. My materials will be what now lies broken at my feet. I must somehow fit those pieces back together. And through it all the question looms, nagging me to quit: "What use are three sided houses anyway?"

The only answer I can find is that they are more use than mounds of rock and ash. I know that even when this place is built it will be imperfect. In time my house will stand among its neighbors, no longer looking lost and ragged. And in fair weather I will look up at that open side more in appreciation of the beauty it once held than in bitterness over what I have lost. But when the clouds roll in that missing wall will leave me open to the rain. Floors and walls will sway and creak in the wind. In the end the best my will and effort can deliver will just make plain how crucial that fourth wall is to make this house complete.

But if it can possibly make sense to you, that is the reason why I must build. I must restore my life because only in that setting can the glory of what I might have had be visible. I must build this flawed, three sided house because it allows me to see how grand was the original when it stood here. His life was such a shining testament to character and courage, if I am to honour his memory I must live by his example.

Variations: The dividing lines between metaphoric stories and some of the other applications discussed in this chapter are necessarily ambiguous, so that a blending of media often conveys a sense of loss more adequately than working in one medium alone. Thus, some persons find that metaphoric stories may grow naturally out of single metaphors, or even drawings that depict the loss in the language of pictures rather than words. Likewise, prose poems may seem like a more congenial form for some persons to explore their grief than narratives in the usual sense, and some persons may even compose representational or abstract music to convey the nature of their grief, taking it as a source of inspiration for creative achievements that might ultimately be shared with others. [13]

Precautions: To an even greater extent than other forms of metaphor, figurative stories should be treated in a respectful rather than analytical fashion by counselors who employ them with their clients. This is because such stories often represent a sense of provisional closure regarding the loss, rather than the more open-ended and shifting imagery in single metaphors. It is therefore more appropriate to inquire gently about the constraints and affordances in the author's account, but without the implication that these can or should be changed in some precipitous fashion. Counselors familiar with projective testing (e.g., the Thematic Apperception Test) will probably be comfortable in soliciting such stories and interrogating their meaning, without imposition of the counselor's own plot structure on the material provided by the author.

A Metaphoric Story of My Loss

_____
_____
_____
_____
_____
_____
_____
_____
_____
_____
_____
_____
_____

What happened before the events in this story? What led up to this part
of the narrative?

_____
_____
_____
_____
_____
_____
_____

What is happening here, from the perspective of each of the characters?
How might each experience this story differently?

_____
_____
_____
_____
_____
_____

What is likely to happen in the future, if this story is to be continued?

_____

_____

_____

_____

_____

_____

_____

What form would growth take in this story, if it would occur? Who would support a change in this direction?

_____

_____

_____

_____

_____

_____

_____

Personal Pilgrimage

Indications: Sometimes in the wake of loss we feel a need to reestablish continuity with persons, places, or traditions that have grown distant and disconnected from our current lives. For example, the death of an older relative in the community in which we were raised can occasion a trip of rediscovery to places that were important to us in childhood, but which we have not visited for much of our adult life. Or we may plan to visit the Vietnam War Memorial or American Holocaust Museum in Washington to restore our sense of connection to lost loved ones or ancestors, even those we never actually met. In any of these cases, the experience can be profound, calling forth or creating memories and emotions that deepen our sense of our own place in the history of our family or our people.

Example: When she turned forty, something in Maria told her she needed to seek out her roots, and reconnect her life more firmly to a history that had previously seemed irrelevant to her life. Recently divorced and with grown children, Maria had been born into a Native American family that moved from the New Mexican pueblo where she spent her first year to a large southwestern city in pursuit of greater educational and occupational opportunity. Much of her people's culture was left behind in the move, and the rest was gradually eroded as Maria pursued her own higher education in another state. There she married, raised her own children, and made only periodic visits to her parents in their urban home.

But somehow, Maria's divorce prompted her to return to New Mexico, not merely to her parent's home, but also to the pueblo of her birth and several other culturally and spiritually significant sites—some archeological, some inhabited—that represented the history of her people. What began as a trip became a "vision quest," which involved her studying with elders of her tribe, and researching and participating in nearly lost traditions. This quest, distributed across several trips over a period of years, deepened her spirituality, reconnected her with her tradition, and allowed her to rediscover and cultivate a set of values and life philosophy that had "gotten lost in the shuffle" of her mobile middle class existence.

Variations: Pilgrimages can be as humble as a drive to one's home town, or as ambitious as extended travel to one's ancestral homeland. Likewise, they can be as mundane as revisiting the drugstore that your father used to own and in which you spent countless hours as a child, or as sacred as Maria's vision quest. When actual travel to a place of significance is impossible, some sense of reconnection can nonetheless be established by reading pictorial histories of its people, or researching newspaper archives that chronicled important events and personalities who provided a context for the development of your own identity. Whatever the form of pilgrimage, its significance can be enhanced by augmenting it with a personal journal that captures the impressions, recollections, and emotions triggered by the experience.

Precautions: While some pilgrimages can be joyful adventures of rediscovery, others can involve disillusionment and even heartbreak, as when a Jewish person visits the camp at Auschwitz where his grandparents were killed. For this reason, planning for such travel should attend to the emotional as well as pragmatic dimensions of the trip, such as the decision to go alone or with a friend or relative, how and where one will find the reflective time to process the experience, etc. Pilgrims also need to be prepared for the possibility that the trip will not yield any epiphany, but instead may raise more troubling questions than it resolves. As a way of knitting together the "times of our lives," however, the personal pilgrimage can be a powerful means of transforming loss into gain.

Photo Gallery

Indications: Photographs, perhaps more than any other form of memento, provide vivid ways of memorializing the lives of those we have loved. At least as important as their private function in fostering our symbolic connection to a person who has died, is their public function in prompting shared reminiscence about that person. Bereaved parents in particular may find photographs a natural way to "introduce" their lost children to others in their lives, and to promote spontaneous storytelling that both vivifies memories and validates their status as parents. [14]

There are many ways in which snapshots can be used to celebrate a life and preserve its significance for our own, ranging from keeping photos of lost loved ones in one's wallet or at natural places of conversation in the home, to creating more elaborate collages or albums memorializing their entire lives or our special relationship to them. Once assembled, such photo galleries can be drawn upon to facilitate reminiscence at special moments (e.g., the anniversary of the person's birth or death) or to stimulate collective remembering at memorial ceremonies or less formal occasions.

Example: Bob and Janet sought marital counseling for a number of problems in their relationship, including mutual problems with anger control, career indecision, difficulty "communicating," and a shifting litany of weekly complaints that made it hard to make much progress on any one of them. The one recurrent theme in their "fights" was a struggle over Beau, Janet's fourteen-year old Labrador retriever, whose advanced age had left him in obvious pain, with limited mobility, and frequent problems with incontinence. Virtually every session Bob would "rationally" argue that the dog (whose relationship with Janet was longer and probably less ambivalent than his own) be "put to sleep for his own good," to which Janet would respond emotionally, attacking Bob's callousness. Flare-ups were especially likely when sessions followed an evening when Beau would climb into bed with the couple, become incontinent, and be kicked to the floor by an angry Bob.

Numerous attempts at negotiating the conflict failed, until I inquired about the couple's history of loss. Somewhat surprised, Janet related two important episodes, one involving the miscarriage of their hoped for child a few years before, to which Bob had proven indifferent, and a second involving the stillbirth of a second baby, to which he responded with compassion and understanding, even using his considerable skills as a photographer to take pictures of the baby in his mother's arms prior to burial. Both spouses were visibly moved by this discussion, leading me to ask whether Bob could play a similar role with their "surviving child," Beau, and take some professional quality photographs of him with Janet, in view of his uncertain health and longevity. In return, I wondered aloud whether Janet could use her skills as a carpenter to construct a suitable bed for Beau (complete with waterproof mattress!) to avert problems with his sharing their bed. Somewhat warily at first, both partners discussed the idea and agreed to the plan.

Our next session, two weeks later, was a powerful contrast to those that had come before. In place of the usual distance and accusations, Bob and Janet sat snuggled up on the couch, arms around each other, talking quietly and proudly about their newfound intimacy. When I inquired about how Beau was doing, Bob replied that Janet, on her own, had made the painful but appropriate decision to have the dog put to sleep a few days before. Janet then explained that the photo assignment had "been the key that opened the door," as Bob not only took memorial photos of the dog, but had constructed an entire collage of his life, from his puppyhood catching Frisbees in the park through his maturity and old age. Both spouses shed a few quiet tears and embraced, sharing the opinion that they would need only a few more sessions of counseling to resolve their remaining issues.

Variations: A colleague of mine recently compiled a calendar featuring her deceased pre-school son, with each monthly page being introduced by a photograph depicting him at that season of the year: hunting for Easter eggs in April, playing in the pool in July, dressed in Halloween garb in October, and joyfully unwrapping presents at Christmas time. She then had it duplicated at a local copy store as a gift to her husband, for whom it provides warm monthly reminders of the way in which a delightful little imp had graced their lives together for too few years.

This past Christmas I also compiled a few old home movies of my childhood prior to my father's death, and had them transferred to a videotape format, giving copies to my mother, sister, and brother, who had not seen them for decades. This gift of family history was especially relevant to my brother, as the movies dated from a time when he was the age of his younger son, to the time he was the age of his older boy. Developing technologies permit more and more experimentation with the images of lost loved ones, as illustrated by the bereaved father who decided to scan several photos of his little girl to have pop up spontaneously as the screen saver on his home computer.

Precautions: Constructing a photo collage or one of its variations can be daunting if you take it as an assignment to "tell the whole story" of your subject's life, so that it is usually better to have humbler ambitions. Because of the power of images to recapture lost moments, expressions, and activities, it can also be emotionally intense, and for this reason may best be pursued in manageable doses. Remember that the process of constructing a photographic memorial is as important as the product, so that pausing to savor the experience, discuss it with a friend or counselor, and perhaps even keep a journal of your reactions and recollections along the way can add another dimension to this application.

Poetry of Loss

Indications: Literal language fails to capture the nuances of feeling and meaning that constitute our unique sense of loss. Poetic self-expression presses back the boundaries of public speech, articulating symbolically what cannot be stated plainly. Writing personal poetry, for no audience other than yourself, can sometimes help crystallize a moment, validate an emotion, or convey a felt sense in a way that straightforward writing cannot. Abandon a concern with form and rhyme, and pen a few lines that capture an aspect of your experience without concern for editing them for public sharing.

Example: On a recent, brilliant fall morning, I noticed a curious edge of sadness as I strolled outside, momentarily free of other responsibilities. Reflecting for a moment, I quickly traced the sadness to the absence of someone I loved, and sat down to write the following simple poem, which honored the fleeting sense of loss and the relationship to which it referred.

The Shadow of Your Absence

I wanted to share with you
The colors of this day.
But in the shadow of your absence
They faded
Before I had the chance.

The poetry of loss can be highly individualized, or speak to nearly universal aspects of human experience. It can be in virtually any form, from metaphoric prose to rhythmic incantations, and can illuminate a single feeling (anger, desolation, hope) or summarize the essence of an entire relationship. Nessa Rapoport's 1994 volume, *A Woman's Book of Grieving* (New York: William Morrow) gives some idea of the many forms that such poetic reflections might take.

Variations: Counselors may sometimes feel moved to respond in a nonliteral way to a client's poetic productions, in a sense honoring the risk the client has taken by setting aside the usual constraints and writing a response from the heart. For example, a few months ago a young man who was in training to become a counselor shared with me a series of evocative prose poems, following a tearful and poignant session with me in which he acknowledged his misgivings about his chosen career. In his writing he lamented the loss of a spontaneous, playful, genuine, and more emotional part of himself, which he felt had been buried beneath the sometimes suffocating requirements to be self-controlled, efficient, cautious, and intellectual fostered by his graduate training. The loss of his earlier self had been gradual, but the recognition of it was abrupt, and the force of it triggered an outpouring of feeling that could appropriately be described as grief.

As I was moved and touched by his risk-taking, I responded in kind, writing him a brief poem that attempted to capture the essence of his struggle, but suggest the hopeful resolution that I felt deeply was possible for him:

Fragments

Like echoes of voices long silent or sleeping,
these cries and whispers murmur still,
disturbing the sedimented practices
that muffle their disquiet in layers of convention.

And yet, they emerge again from their slumbers
when storms or gentle rains erode their anonymous shroud of years,
and give clues to the larger pattern of coherence that once was theirs,
and may yet be again.

Precautions: Like any form of creative endeavor, poetic self-expression is a skill that is refined over time, and one that may benefit from critique by a suitable mentor. But in its therapeutic rather than artistic use, it need not be refined in order to be effective in speaking from the bereaved person's experience, and perhaps even in speaking to the losses of others. Thus, it is important that the counselor (or author for that matter) not adopt the role of a critical editor attempting to "improve" the work, but instead take the position of an explorer attempting to enter into the world of feeling evoked by the poem, in order to explore its dimensions. If the counselor has not built a foundation of deep respect for the client's offerings, whether oral or written, then encouragement to share such poetry in the context of counseling is inappropriate and should be avoided.

My poem(s) of loss

Title:

_____
_____
_____
_____
_____
_____
_____
_____
_____

Title:

_____
_____
_____
_____
_____
_____
_____
_____

Title:

_____
_____
_____
_____
_____
_____
_____

Reflective Reading

Indications: Grief can be an isolating and sometimes incomprehensible experience. For this very reason, reading about others' experiences of mourning in a way that helps interpret it can both be a comfort to the grieving individual, and help structure a compelling but confusing transition. Several suitable books on grief and loss issues exist in the self-help literature, among more spiritually oriented books, or in first-person, fiction or non-fiction accounts (e.g., James Agee's *A Death in the Family*, or C.S. Lewis's *A Grief Observed*). Any of these can make suitable reading for some bereaved persons, as long as they are compatible with that person's preferred reading level, faith tradition (if any), and level of concentration. Numerous examples of books and other print resources are provided in the next chapter.

Variations: In grief therapy, specific chapters from the present book or other sources might be assigned as homework to prompt later in-session discussion, a strategy that might be especially helpful in establishing a common agenda for support groups. Also in groups, members might be encouraged to share readings they have found helpful, which can be compiled into an annotated bibliography for interested persons to consult. Readings can be used easily in conjunction with other exercises, e.g., by reading Chapter 6 on *Ritual and Remembrance* prior to constructing a personal ritual to memorialize one of one's own losses.

Precautions: During the acute stages of grief, bereaved persons may suffer from many of the symptoms of depression, including difficulty with both concentration and memory. Thus, it is especially appropriate that any reading done during this time be brief and focused, so that readers can "dose" the readings with this in mind. The chapters of Part I of the present volume, as well as most of the exercises in this chapter, were written with this need for brevity in mind.

Care also must be taken to avoid prescriptive or pathologizing treatments of loss, whether these are written from a medical, religious, or narrowly theoretical perspective. For example, popular books may frequently simplify grief by imposing upon it the structure of presumed stages, which can then be taken as norms against which clients can judge themselves. It is therefore helpful to approach any such reading with the following questions in mind, which might be discussed openly with a counselor or reflected upon privately by the reader.

Book Title: _____

- In what way did this account of grief correspond to my own experience of loss?

  _____
  _____
  _____
  _____
  _____
  _____

- In what way did it fail to match my experience?

  _____
  _____
  _____
  _____

- What did I learn about loss from reading this book?

  _____
  _____
  _____
  _____

- What words of advice would I give another who was interested in reading this work?

  _____

  _____

  _____

  _____

  _____

  _____

  _____

  _____

- If I had to sum up the gist of this book's message in a sentence, what would it be?

  _____

  _____

  _____

  _____

Ritualization

Indications: As discussed in Part 1 of this book, both the formal and informal ritualization of loss can give meaning to the significant transitions of our lives, while securing a sense of continuity with what came before and what will follow. Effective grief rituals may be private or public, spiritual or secular, but they have in common that they entail some form of *symbolic action* that helps us reaffirm our relationship to that which we have lost, and understand the new identity into which we are introduced as a function of the loss experience. [15] While many bereaved persons find comfort in standard church liturgies and cultural customs of mourning, others find the modification of these standard practices or the construction of wholly original ones of greater value in speaking to their particular form of grief. Personal rituals are especially appropriate when the losses do not stem from a death in the family, such as the "disenfranchised" losses of unconventional relationships, roles, or social statuses discussed in Chapter 4.

Example: Henry, a simple man who fathered a loving family, had lived long and well, raising five children with his wife on their Nebraska farm. When he died suddenly of heart failure in his early 80's, his grown children and grandchildren returned to the family home to help his mother sort things out, and make the transition into a smaller home that required less upkeep. As they cleaned out his well-used wood shop, they discovered a box of partially finished carvings—of birds, animals, and children's toys—that provided mute but eloquent testimony to his many years of passionate "whittling." In a moment of inspiration, his oldest son suggested that they incorporate the unfinished carvings, along with several of his completed ones, into his memorial service. As family members, young and old, came forward to reminisce about their father, grandfather, or brother, they associated it to a carving they carried that had some special significance to them. The carvings were then placed on a large display board and given to Henry's wife, for whom it symbolized much of what her husband had cared about, and the ways in which he had touched so many through his craftsmanship and through his life.

Variations: Memorial ceremonies can be adapted to the circumstances of the mourners in numerous ways, just as other ritual occasions can provide opportunities for memorialization. Illustrations of the former could be the sponsorship of a candlelight prayer service for survivors of suicide at a professional meeting on the topic, or the dedication of a bench or small garden in honor of a faculty member who had long served in a given academic department. Examples of the latter would include reserving a space for a deceased parent in the front row of one's wedding service, or donating a toy to charity at Christmas time in the name of a deceased child. The key to either kind of memorialization is sensitivity not only to the memory of lost loved ones, but also to the unique needs and preferences of survivors.

Rituals can take many forms in addition to the sort of public observance illustrated above. For example, families may create their own domestic rituals, perhaps taking off work and school on the birthday of a child who died, simply to spend the day doing something enjoyable together. Or individuals might use standard ritual forms for private purposes, such as literally burying a symbolic reminder of a destructive childhood, or drafting a personal "Declaration of Independence" from a relationship that has become oppressive. [16] Because these smaller scale observances need to meet only the needs of a few individuals (or even one), mourners using them can take greater risks with powerful symbolic statements or actions that need not even "make sense" to the outside observer.

Precautions: In planning public observances, it is important to guard against a "uniformity myth," presuming that a single ritual form will meet the needs of all persons equally well. For this reason, it is important to discuss the planned ceremony with others who can be expected to take part in it. Encouraging creative input on the part of all participants can help promote a sense of shared "ownership" of the ritual, enhancing its value in reaffirming relationships among survivors.

In constructing private rituals, it is particularly important to assess the timing and appropriateness of the form of memorialization in relation to the survivor's needs in the moment. For example, a poorly timed recommendation on the part of a counselor that a grieving client take symbolic action to "say good-bye" to a lost loved one can be resisted as forcing premature closure to a relationship that requires greater "sifting through" to feel complete. Likewise, the most effective rituals may arise as inspirations or spontaneous enactments rather than highly planful activities, as when a round of shared reminiscence about a lost loved one at a family gathering leads to a joint decision to prepare and share a favorite dish of the deceased at dinner that evening. Especially as the raw event of the loss grows more distant with the passing of time, ritual observances can come to be marked by laughter as well as tears, challenging the assumption that they must necessarily be solemn occasions.

The loss I want to ritualize is:

_____

_____

_____

_____

The ritual I would like to plan would involve:

_____

_____

_____

_____

_____

_____

_____

_____

_____

The role of other people in this ritual (if any), would be:

_____

_____

_____

_____

_____

_____

Unsent Letters

Indications: One of the most popular forms of therapeutic writing in the wake of loss is the "unsent letter," a written message to the deceased that expresses some of what could not be expressed prior to that person's death. Such letters are especially useful when the griever carries a burden of resentment or guilt that is difficult to share with others, but which tends to keep him or her locked into an emotional preoccupation with the death, and perhaps the many other indirect losses that preceded it. Though simple, the suggestion to pour out one's heart in the form of an unsent missive can prove therapeutically powerful, whether or not it is incorporated into a formal course of grief counseling or therapy.

Example: Karen, whose son Kenny died after eight difficult years of profound physical and mental disability, sought grief therapy when she felt "stuck" in her bereavement several months after his death. What was especially worrisome to her was her tendency to "cut herself off from everybody," because as she said, "everybody had let her down" during her son's lifetime. Karen was also troubled by Kenny's "slipping away during the night" during his last hospitalization, while she was at home with her remaining child. This sense of guilt was made more keen by her decision during the final months of Kenny's life to begin dating again, two years after the death of her husband in a vehicular accident, as being out of the home one evening each week left Kenny in the care of others. Although Karen had made considerable progress in her six previous sessions of therapy, she began to identify "unfinished business" with her son, and accepted my suggestion that she "reopen the communication with him" through writing the following unsent letter as therapeutic "homework":

Dear Kenny,
Since you died, there hasn't been a day I have not thought about you. You come to me in my dreams, my thoughts, and my conversations with other people. I see you with your toys, in your wheelchair (which we gave away yesterday), and coming down the ramp to the back porch. But I also feel a distance from you, like I've been holding something back that was too hard to talk about, even with myself. You see, I feel terribly guilty about the way you died.

I think you know how hard my life has been for me since you came to us, but how much I loved you despite it all. Many times I was the only one who could comfort you when you were upset, or who could understand what you wanted when you tried hard to get something across, but couldn't. Being your mom was a 20 hour a day job for me, especially when no one else stepped in to help, or when they quickly left when you protested and wanted only me. God knows, I knew first hand how demanding caring for you could be, and I can't really blame them for wanting to back away. Little by little, you became my whole world, and I let go of other relationships. I guess I was so burnt out for so many years that I didn't even want to have conversations about my thoughts or feelings, anything that would make me more aware of my loneliness. Yet, now that you're gone, I find that the loneliness is even greater, and I've burnt the bridges to other people who once cared about me. I guess I'm trying to figure out, at age 42, how to restart my life.

When you were hospitalized for the last time with pneumonia, I assumed that you would pull through like you had so many times before. Somehow, even though the doctors predicted that you would not live to age 2, God kept performing miracles and you kept struggling back. But when the complications came, and it looked like you would lose all ability to communicate, and maybe even think, I knew the end was coming. I'm sorry, so sorry, if my [DNR] decision was wrong, but it felt even more wrong to keep holding on, when your soul had already left. I guess it is to that soul that I am writing now for forgiveness and understanding.

You may be gone from this house, from your chair, and from your bed, but you will always live in my heart. I will never leave you.

Love,
Mom

Writing this letter, and reading it aloud to me in therapy, was a moving experience for Karen, as well as for me. We discussed those passages that triggered tears (writing to his soul, affirming that she would never leave), as well as how she felt her son would respond (with acceptance and reciprocated love). What was equally powerful was the way in which deciding to write the letter had somehow facilitated her reaching out again to others, as evidenced by her spontaneous phone call to the man she had begun dating, but then stopped seeing when Kenny had died, her inviting her out-of-state mother for a visit, and her phoning a disabled children's organization to donate her son's wheelchair and other medical equipment for the use of others. I reflected for Karen that the theme running through all of these exceptional actions was "reconnecting with others" rather than "pushing away," an interpretation that she reaffirmed. As she stated, "the stress I experienced was not in making the calls, it was in maintaining the distance." Reconnecting with her son thereby served as an avenue for reconnecting with a world of caring others, who both understood some of the chapters of her past, and were willing to help coauthor her future.

Variations: A single unsent letter can often initiate an ongoing "correspondence," with subsequent letters written on significant anniversary dates, or across the course of therapy to track changes in the "relationship" of the bereaved person to his or her lost loved one over time. [17] Moreover, letters *to* the deceased person can be alternated with letters *from* them, written by the grieving person as she or he thinks the lost loved one would respond. If used in the context of grief therapy, this sort of "homework" can be supplemented by Gestalt "two-chair" work, in which the client is asked to successively take the perspective of self and loved one and carry on the conversation that was interrupted by death. [18]

A simple but touching variation on the unsent letter involves visiting a card shop and selecting the card a deceased loved one would choose for you on a special occasion (Mother's Day, your birthday), and then send it to yourself. The act of selecting a card on his or her behalf can be as significant a gesture as mailing and receiving the greeting.

Finally, nothing dictates that unsent letters be used only in connection with typical bereavement. For example, drafting a statement of one's feelings or summarizing one's present status may be equally relevant in cases of divorce or job loss, when the addressee might be one's previous spouse, partner, or employer. Particularly when the leave-taking has been abrupt and involuntary, a good deal may remain to be processed in these forms of loss, and unsent letters may provide a step in this direction.

Precautions: Too often, grieving persons and their counselors make use of unsent letters in the mistaken belief that they will "finish the unfinished business" in a complicated relationship, and perhaps allow the person to "close the book" on his or her mourning altogether. However, unsent letters might better be seen as ways of *reopening the conversation,* rather than *closing it,* with its implication for "resolving" the relationship "once and for all." Thus, like other narrative techniques outlined in this chapter, they provide structures for sifting through complex experiences of loss, rather than magical panaceas for eliminating the inevitable pain entailed by significant life transitions.

A final caveat concerns the title of this application, namely that the letter be *unsent* (at least to another person). Except in rare instances, the therapeutic value of this form of expressive writing is not increased by stamping and posting such letters to other parties, especially those we feel have wronged us (as in the case of a contentious divorce or wrongful dismissal). If the intent is healing oneself rather than seeking retribution with others, then such letters are likely to help us gain personal perspective on some of the issues arising from our loss, as well as those that demand further attention.

Conclusion

Grieving has often been likened to a journey, conveying the sense that one enters it at one place, and moves through a desolate and unfamiliar terrain before returning, with luck, to a place near one's point of origin. In traditional grief theory, the journey is implicitly assumed to be a private one, undertaken by a solitary traveler, who finds his or her way using familiar guideposts that signal each new stage of the trip. This conventional approach offers the bereaved individual the comfort of a clear road map through previously unexplored territory, though with an accompanying warning that diversions from the recommended route represent dubious detours at best, and dangerous dead-ends at worst. Grief counselors, in this view, function as travel consultants who quickly assess the bereaved individual's needs and resources, and suggest an itinerary from a limited guidebook of options that efficiently keep the person moving toward the journey's preordained conclusion.

In the meaning making model developed here, the journey of grieving is quite a different one. Loss, in this view, forces the unbidden exploration of a new, if initially painful world, on a boundless journey from which we will never completely return. In the course of our travels we will be confronted by innumerable choices, some apparently trivial, others existentially consequential, but none of which can be easily resolved by consulting a standard guidebook. Gone is the comforting familiarity of universal guideposts, but gone too is the implication that the twists and turns of our personal journey represent dangerous deviations to be diagnosed or distrusted. Moreover, while appreciating that each traveler ultimately experiences a different landscape, this approach to mourning emphasizes the joint role of others in shaping the direction and pace of our journey, whether these others are members of our intimate circle of family and friends, or represent fellow travelers encountered along the way. The grief counselor too, in this view, acts as a fellow traveler rather than consultant, sharing the uncertainties of the journey, and walking alongside, rather than leading the grieving individual along the unpredictable road toward a new adaptation.

One goal of this book has been to offer some rough sketches of the possible terrain that grieving persons may encounter, whether the losses they have sustained result from the death of loved ones or other unwelcome transitions encountered in the course of living and relating. Beyond this, however, I have tried to offer a view of mourning as a process of *meaning reconstruction,* a view that is consonant with the "growing edge" of contemporary grief theory. In particular, I hope that the ideas offered here sensitize the reader to the more subtle dimensions of loss that have too long been obscured beneath simplistic models, and that the applications of these ideas will encourage and hearten the traveler on his or her personal journey through grieving.

Chapter 9 Research Notes

1. Readers interested in learning more about constructivist and narrative approaches to psychotherapy can consult R. A. Neimeyer & M. J. Mahoney (Eds.) (1995), *Constructivism in psychotherapy*, Washington, D.C.: American Psychological Association, and J. B. Eron and T. W. Lund (1996), *Narrative solutions in brief therapy*, New York: Guilford, for useful introductions.

2. Other narrative strategies (e.g., journals, poetry) used by Carol to address the losses of her life are detailed in R. A. Neimeyer (1995). Client-generated narratives in psychotherapy. In R. A. Neimeyer & M. J. Mahoney (Eds.) (1995), *Constructivism in psychotherapy*, Washington, D.C.: American Psychological Association.

3. A more elaborate variation of this application is to conduct a "life review project," by noting each year of your life on a large note card or sheet of paper, and then writing significant events associated with each on the corresponding card. As in the biographies described here, other informants can be consulted to help fill in details, resulting in something between the "chapter heading" exercise illustrated in this chapter and a full narrative autobiography. Clinically oriented readers may wish to consult M. J. Mahoney (1991), *Human change processes*. New York: Basic Books, for details.

More academic readers may want to explore the fascinating emerging literature in *ethnography* and *autoethnography*, a vein of qualitative research that attempts to bring to light the "culture" of particular persons and groups, including various "cultures" defined by a shared loss. Excellent illustrations include Michelle Miller's (1995) article, An intergenerational case study of suicidal tradition and mother-daughter communication, *Journal of Applied Communication Research, 23,* 247-270, and Dennis Klass's (1997) The deceased child in the psychic and social worlds of bereaved parents during the resolution of grief, *Death Studies, 21,* 147-175. The best introduction to this genre of research has been provided by Carolyn Ellis and Arthur Bochner (Eds.) (1996), *Composing ethnography*. Walnut Creek, CA: Alta Mira (a division of Sage). The book contains several engrossing and often disturbing examples of authors coping with various kinds of loss, with an emphasis on how these have shaped their identities.

4. Of course, drawings of death and loss may be especially valuable for those persons, such as children, who may be less able to express the nuances of their feelings and meanings in verbal form. As stressed below, if one approaches such productions with curiosity rather than conclusions, drawings can open a door to substantial dialogue about their significance even with artists as young as three or four. Death-related art work can also be the subject for serious scientific study, as in the elegant research by M. E. Tamm and A. Granqvist (1995), The meaning of death for children and adolescents: A phenomenographic study of drawings. *Death Studies, 19,* 203-222. These investigators invited a large, carefully stratified sample of Swedish school children to depict "death," and conducted a thematic analysis of the resulting drawings to identify reliable age- and gender-related trends. Thus, while my emphasis in the present volume is practical more than scholarly, it is worth noting that there is nothing intrinsically "unscientific" about a focus on meanings rather than "objective" symptoms as a pathway to understanding the psychology of death and loss.

5. An instructive precaution about the condensation of personal meaning in an epitaph can be derived from the emotionally evocative masterpiece by James Agee (1938/1985), *A death in the family,* New York: Bantam. In one scene, Mary, whose husband Jay has just died suddenly in his prime in an auto accident, seizes on a consoling expression of her brother, who underscored her husband's apparent physical and psychological strength at the moment of his death. Mary, struggling valiantly to find meaning in a seemingly meaningless tragedy, spontaneously and earnestly suggests that "In his strength" be used as an apt epitaph for his tombstone. Several other family members enthusiastically support the idea before Mary's nearly deaf mother learns the gist of the discussion, and questions whether something with so private a meaning would be suitable in so public a place as a graveyard. Though she tries to disguise her disappointment, Mary is crushed, and after a brief effort to persuade her mother, lets to idea die, wishing she had never suggested it. Ironically, to the extent that bereaved persons find a particular

epitaph uniquely meaningful, they may have to contend with the possibility that this meaning might not be widely understood, even by those who know them intimately.

6. The most important program of research substantiating this impressive claim has been provided by James Pennebaker and his colleagues at Southern Methodist University. In dozens of studies of expressive journalling, they provide persuasive evidence for the healing power of "confessing" one's deepest secrets, even in the context of research in which confidentiality is protected by anonymity. The results of these studies, along with a broader consideration of the role of disclosure of trauma in religious, secular, and laboratory settings, is presented in Pennebaker's (1997) book, *Opening up*, New York: Guilford. The guidelines regarding the use of therapeutic journalling provided below represent modifications and extensions of his basic instructional set.

7. An excellent introduction to using journals to promote self-awareness and personal growth is Tristine Rainer's (1978) book, *The new diary*. Los Angeles: Tarcher. She provides apt advice on nearly every aspect of journal work, from selecting a diary to arranging for privacy, and from experimenting with different "voices" to writing with different intentions. It will prove accessible and useful to individuals interested in using the method, as well as professional counselors interested in incorporating it into their work.

8. The life imprint technique, along with related means of fostering continued connection to lost loved ones, was suggested by Craig Vickio (1998) in his article "Together in spirit: Keeping our relationships alive when loved ones die." *Death Studies*, in press.

9. Psychoanalytic writers in particular have focused on the pathological implications of identification with the deceased, in keeping with their model of mourning as the painful but necessary relinquishment of attachment. However, newer thinking within this tradition is recognizing the potential healthiness of positive identification with those we have lost, just as it is questioning the long-held dogma that one needs to disengage from the

deceased in order to reinvest one's energies elsewhere. For an intelligent discussion of this "new look" in analysis, see George Hagman's (1995) paper entitled "Mourning: A review and reconsideration," *International Journal of Psycho-Analysis, 76,* 909-925.

10. The Loss Characterization represents an adaptation of the Self-Characterization method introduced by George Kelly (1955), in his book, *The psychology of personal constructs,* New York: Norton. I have likewise adapted his suggestions for interpreting such sketches to the particular case of loss. Readers interested in learning more about the use of this and other constructivist methods in the counseling context may wish to read R. A. Neimeyer (1993), Constructivist approaches to the measurement of meaning. In G. J. Neimeyer (Ed.), *Constructivist assessment.* Newbury Park: Sage.

11. Some of these prompts are derived from those contained in the "Cherished Memories" album distributed by the Grieving Well Center, P.O. Box 622256, Orlando, FL, 32862-2256. Their commercially available album is lavishly formatted, and might make a thoughtful gift for a bereaved person, in addition to a thought-provoking "self help" strategy.

12. Unlike most other clinical vignettes used in this book, in which I have taken precautions to protect the identities of the persons involved, Steve's identity is "real." He granted permission for his account to be included in this book in the hope that he could speak to others who shared the anguish of being bereaved parents, and that he could convey his belief that rebuilding one's life, while painful, was none the less possible. I would like to publicly express my appreciation to Steve for his courage and perspicacity, and to my colleague and friend Stephen Fleming for making me aware of Steve's moving narrative.

13. A particularly moving example of music inspired by grief is the Survivors' Symphony, a piece commissioned by the Association for Death Education and Counseling (ADEC), composed by Douglas Lofstrom, and performed by full orchestra. Readers interested in obtaining an inexpensive

cassette recording of this stirring performance can contact ADEC at (860) 586-7503 or by e-mail at info@adec.org.

14. An eloquent piece of qualitative research that documents and extends these claims has been authored by Gordon Riches and Pamela Dawson (1998), entitled Lost Children, Living Memories: The Role of Photographs in Processes of Grief and Adjustment Among Bereaved Parents, *Death Studies, 22*, in press. These investigators vividly illustrate how snapshots and other artifacts are recruited by parents to serve a number of psychologically significant functions, although their value is often overlooked by grief theorists, researchers, and therapists.

15. For an intelligent discussion of this view of ritualization, see Bronna Romanoff and Marion Terenzio (1998), Rituals and the grieving process, *Death Studies, 22*, in press.

16. This suggestion conforms to a narrative model of therapy, which creatively uses therapist as well as client-generated documents to affirm and support clients' resistance against "dominant narratives" that subjugate them to unwanted or negative identities. For a conceptual rationale and practical illustrations, see Michael White an David Epston (1990). *Narrative means to therapeutic ends.* New York: Norton.

17. An informative example of such continued correspondence emerged in a spontaneous grief journal kept by a young woman whose father had died, which was given to a team of bereavement researchers in the course of a formal study. The author's entries, each of which began with "Dear Dad," and ended with "Love, Rhonda," vividly traced changes in her continuing relationship to his memory, and documented the life lessons she had learned from him and from his death. For details, see David Balk and Laura Vesta (1998), Psychological development during four years of bereavement: A longitudinal case study. *Death Studies, 22*, 23-41.

18. Professionals interested in a videotaped demonstration of such two chair work in a case of grieving can contact The Master Therapists Program, Dept. of Psychiatry/CME, University of Connecticut Health Center, 263 Farmington Avenue, Farmington, CT 06030-2945 (860) 679-3789, and request information on ordering tape #43-96 (Neimeyer), entitled *Death, loss, and personal reconstruction.*

Chapter 10

Resources for Further Exploration

There are many books, organizations, and Web resources available that address themes of death and loss, from scholarly as well as applied perspectives. A few of the best are presented below as further resources for personal or professional education.

ssional literature

Adams, D.W. & Deveau, E.J. (1988). *Coping with childhood cancer.* Hamilton, Ontario: Kinbrigde Publications.

Attig, T. (1996). *How we grieve: Relearning the world.* New York: Oxford University Press.

Death Studies [Professional journal covering literature in all aspects of death and bereavement]. Philadelphia: Taylor & Francis.

Doka, K. J. (1993). *Death and spirituality.* Amityville, NY: Baywood.

Doka, K. J. (1996). *Living with grief after sudden loss.* Washington: Hospice Foundation of America.

Doka, K. J. (1997). *Living with grief when illness is prolonged.* Washington: Hospice Foundation of America.

Doka, K. J. (1998). *Living with grief: Who we are and how we grieve.* Washington: Hospice Foundation of America.

Horowitz, M. J. (1997). *Stress response syndromes.* Northvale, NJ: Jason Aronson.

Journal of Personal and Interpersonal Loss [Professional journal covering a diverse literature on loss, especially from a social psychological stand point]. Philadelphia: Taylor & Francis.

Leenaars, A. A. (Ed.) (1993). *Suicidology.* Northvale, NJ: Jason Aronson.

Leenaars, A. A., Maltsberger, J.T., & Neimeyer, R.A. (Eds.) (1994). *Treatment of suicidal people.* Philadelphia: Taylor & Francis.

Neimeyer, R. A. (1997). *Death anxiety handbook.* Philadelphia: Taylor & Francis.

Nord, D. (1997). *Multiple AIDS-related loss.* Philadelphia: Taylor & Francis.

Omega: Journal of Death and Dying [Professional journal dealing with research on death attitudes, grief, and related areas]. Amityville, NY: Baywood.

Rando, T. A. (1993). *Treatment of complicated mourning.* Champaign, IL: Research Press.

Strack, S. (1997). *Death and the quest for meaning.* Northvale, NJ: Jason Aronson.

Stroebe, M.S., Stroebe, W. & Hansson, R. O. (Eds.) (1993). *Handbook of bereavement.* Cambridge, England: Cambridge University Press.

Viney, L. L. (1989). *Images of illness* (2nd ed.). Malabar, FL: Krieger.

Walsh, R. & McGoldrick, M. (Eds.) (1991). *Living beyond loss: Death in the family.* New York: Norton.

Wass, H. & Neimeyer, R. A. (Eds.). (1995). *Dying: Facing the facts.* Philadelphia: Taylor & Francis.

Worden, J. W. (1991). *Grief counseling and grief therapy.* New York: Springer.

Worden, J. A. (1996). *Children and grief: When a parent dies.* New York: Guilford.

Books for Lay Readers

Attig, T. (1996). *How we grieve: Relearning the world.* New York: Oxford University Press. [for adults]

Breebaart, J. & Breebaart, P. (1993). *When I die, will I get better?* New York: Peter Bedrick. [for adolescents]

Carrick, C. (1981). *The accident.* New York: Clarion. [for children]

Dodge, N.C. (1986). *Thumpy's story.* [for preschoolers]

Feinstein, D. & Elliot Mayo, P. (1990). *Rituals for living and dying.* San Francisco: Harper. [for adults]

raser, L. (1994)., *Water from the rock: Finding grace in time of loss.* New York: Paulist Press. [for adults]

Grollman, E. (1976). *Talking about death: A dialogue between parent and child.* Boston: Beacon. [for adults]

Harper, G. L. (1992). *Living with dying: Finding meaning in chronic illness.* Grand Rapids, MI: Eerdmans. [for adults]

Harvey, J. (1996). *Embracing their memory: Loss and the social psychology of story telling.* New York: Allyn & Bacon. [for adults]

White, E. B. (1952). *Charlotte's web.* New York: Harper & Row [for children]

net Resources

With the rapid development of the World Wide Web, users now have access to a virtually unlimited network of resources to meet their informational, social support, commemorative, referral, educational, and professional needs. While these sites may not replace the critical role of human contact in the case of either the bereaved or those who help them, they can be a valuable supplement for both sets of potential users. Some of the better resources available on the Web are listed below. [1] However, please note that the ease with which home pages come and go on the Web means that these addresses may quickly change, may be augmented by others, or may be discontinued altogether. For this reason, searching the Internet with such search engines as Netscape Navigator or Microsoft's Internet Explorer using relevant key words (e.g., grief, suicide, cancer) should reveal a host of alternative sites that should be of interest.

Cancer-related

CancerNet: http://www.ncc.go.jp/cnet.html

OncoLink: http://www.oncolink.upenn.edu

Pediatric Art Gallery:
http://www.oncolink.upenn.edu/images/child/gallery3.html

Computer-mediated discussion with professionals
Dr. John Grohol's Mental Health Page: http://www.grohol.com

Sites with multiple hotlinks
Bereavement and Hospice Support Netline:
      http://www.ubalt.edu/www/bereavement
GriefNet: http://www.funeral.net/info/brvres.html
Yahoo's Death Page: http://www.yahoo.com/Society_and_Culture/Death
Webster: http://www.katsden.com/death/index.html

Commemorative sites
A Place to Honor Grief: http://www.webhealing.com
World Wide Cemetary: http://www.interlog.com/~cemetary

Funerals and memorialization
Internet cremation society: http://www.cremation.org
Memorial Gallery Online Catalogue: http://www.grief.com/order.html

Death education
Grief as a family process course: http://www.indiana.edu/~hperf558
Interactive bereavement courses: http://www.bereavement.or/index.html

Professional resources
Association for Death Education and Counseling: http://www.adec.org

Organizations

The following organizations deal with issues of death and loss in its various forms, and frequently can provide information about specialized professional training, useful publications, and self-help groups in your area.

American Association of Suicidology, 2459 South Ash, Denver, CO 80222
American Cancer Society, 1599 Clifton Road NE, Atlanta, GA 30329.

sociation for Death Education and Counseling, 638 Prospect Avenue, Hartford, CT 06105-4298.

enters for Disease Control, National AIDS Clearinghouse, P.O. Box 6003, Rockville, MD 20849-6003.

1ospice Foundation of America, Suite 300, 2001 S Street, NW, Washington, DC 20009.

International Work Group on Death, Dying, and Bereavement, c/o John Morgan, King's College, 266 Epworth Avenue, London, Ontario, Canada, N6A 2M3.

National Association of People with AIDS, 1413 K Street NW, Washington, DC 20005

National Self-Help Clearinghouse, Room 620, 25 West 43rd Street, New York, NY 10036.

Pregnancy and Infant Loss Center, 1421 West Wayzata Blvd., Wayzata, MN 55391.

Society for Compassionate Friends (Bereaved Parents), P.O. Box 3696, Oak Brook, IL 60522-3696.

Chapter 10 Research Notes

1. Most of the sites listed in this section are exerpted from Carla Sof (1997) article, Social support "internetworks," caskets for sale, and mor Thanatology and the information superhighway. *Death Studies, 21,* 553-57